THE TREK
OF
JAMES MacDONALD

NEW CONCORD, OHIO

TO

CALIFORNIA

1850

OREGON - CALIFORNIA TRAIL

Letters of James and Mary McDonald
by Mary Jean [Stoddard] Fowler and
Edgar W. Stanton, III.

Remaining contents of this book by
Edgar W. Stanton, III.

Library of Congress Catalog Card
Number 88-92306
ISBN 0-9621919-0-6

Published by
    Edgar W. Stanton, III
    11476 Larkin Road
    Live Oak, California 95953

Printed in the United States of America

/∙U∙ artprint press
Sacramento, California

11476 Larkin Road
Live Oak, California   95953
January 19, 1988

Dear McDonald Clan!

Time passes as time will and we, the heirs of James and Mary McDonald, have let time remove from our thoughts those great historical events in which our ancestors participated. Today's hustle and bustle of life has become so intense and fast and requires so much of our energies that there is little left to direct our thoughts very far into the past. The future, it seems, is ever so important.

And so it was that for 30 years contents within a booklet containing copies of letters of James and Mary McDonald, written in 1850 during his Trek west to California and authored for the family by a grandson, Dr. Edwin MacDonald Stanton of Schenectady, New York, lay buried in the "attic of my mind".

A few months back I again read this booklet. It truly is a historical document, laid down in the words of my great grandfather as he saw and endured each day of a long and painful and hazardous journey.

The realization that a bit of my heritage lies on the trail of that great movement West - HIS TRAIL - kindled my interest and pride and excitement.

My home is near the California end of the McDonald trail. My recent travels along Idaho's Snake River and Nevada's Humboldt River and to Hangtown and Carson City and Sacramento City and Onion Valley and Marysville have caused me to wonder "at what point in my travels have I crossed his footsteps?".

This addendum does not answer that question exactly, but it does come close and I hope it adds to your knowledge and pleasure and arouses the pride we all must possess to keep the McDonald pioneering spirit alive. So let us travel a bit in our thoughts as we follow in the footsteps of James McDonald 138 years after his great Trek.

Edgar Williams Stanton, III
Grandson of Margaret [Maggie] McDonald Stanton

1. Enclosed are contents of 3 McDonald letters to "Maggie", my Grandmother.
2. The fotos are of places or things found along the McDonald Trail and mentioned in the McDonald letters, or those that he must have witnessed but failed to make comment.   EWS

FORWARD

The GOLD RUSH years of '49 and the early '50s represent the greatest voluntary migration the world has ever known. It was the lure of the riches in the creeks and rivers of California that lead to the "opening up" of that great territory west of the Missouri River to what we have today--a United States from the Atlantic to the Pacific.

This book is about a man who participated in this great movement and contributed his wee bit to the history of that era which, today, effects my life and yours. Perhaps through this publication some little part of that history is preserved.

The contents of this book stem from the letters of **James McDonald** written to his wife while on his journey west by ox-team and covered wagon to California in 1850. The first section of this book is a story of **James McDonald's** trek along the Oregon-California trail from St. Joseph, Missouri to Sacramento City, and told in words and photographs by Edgar W. Stanton, III. It is a true story, not only of James McDonald, but of all those emigrants who suffered through those endless miles with that pot of gold ever in their vision.

The second section contains copies of the original correspondence between James McDonald and his wife, Mary, written during his trek "across the plains" and while in California. It also contains some family history, including a photograph or two. This section has been preserved over the past years in a booklet for family members through courtesy of Dr. Edwin MacDonald Stanton (dec.), senior grandson of James and Mary.

Edgar W. Stanton, III, great grandson of James and Mary.
11476 Larkin Road, Live Oak, California   95953

November 1988

INTRODUCTION AND ACKNOWLEDGMENTS

Following in the footsteps of my great grandfather, James McDonald, had been a thought in the back of my mind for some years. I am no history buff, but I live in an area where the names of some of those early and famous men of California history show up. Our home is on "Larkin" Road, "Sutter" County. "John Sutter" farmed on his "Hock" farm, a little south of here on the "Feather River". "John C. Fremont's" name is on a plaque west of here in the "Sutter Buttes". "James McDonald" served on the "vigilantes Committee" at "Marysville".

The realization that the trail history of this man, James McDonald, was being lost to the passing time guided me into some action toward a recording of his travels through this gold rush period. My wife and companion, Ginger, and I therefore drove to St. Joseph, Missouri, the beginning of the McDonald trail. Our purpose was to follow those footsteps of James McDonald as he described his way to the California gold fields, as documented in letters to his wife, Mary. We would record every place and every thing mentioned in his journal, and some not mentioned. We were 136 years later, but it would be the same rivers and valleys and deserts and mountains through which he traveled.

Our start was to pass through the St. Joseph museum, seeking a possible bit of information. We found that we were about as uninformed as was McDonald as to where we were going and what to expect. Jacqueline Lewin, the museum Curator of History, was kind to us to give us many "pointers" regarding our search for the McDonald Trail. We had in hand a booklet of the McDonald letters authored by Edwin MacDonald Stanton, senior grandson of James and Mary McDonald. We also there obtained two very valuable

books to help us in our search, "Maps of the Oregon Trail" by Gregory M. Franzwa and "Historic Sites Along the Oregon Trail" by Aubrey L. Haines. And so we headed west, with camera in hand, to photograph those things and places mentioned [and some not mentioned] in the McDonald letters.

Our first stop was about 15 miles west of St. Joseph at an Antique Shop located in a little red barn. I there learned how an ox is made and the nomenclature of the parts of an ox yoke. Our learning had begun. We moved westward, stopping at river crossings, trail markers, museums, National Monuments, any where a bit of history might be found and, in particular, those places mentioned in the booklet of McDonald letters. And we talked to people, so many interesting and helpful people. There were museum curators [many fine museums along this track], farmers, service station attendants, store keepers, fellow campers, cowboys, waitresses, game wardens, ranchers, "old timers", rural mail carriers. Some names come to my mind of those along the Trail who aided in our search, Jacqueline Lewin of St. Joseph museum, Louise Samson of Fort Laramie, Mr. Sun of Devils Gate and Sweetwater country, Mrs. Wright of Farson, Wyoming.

This journey of ours along the McDonald Trail started in September of 1986. It was not completed until June of 1988. It includes two more runs [round trip to Fort Kearney] to catch what we missed the first time through. A great part of the story that could have been told in his letters he has omitted. His account does not tell us of the perils encountered. I believe he did not want to alarm his wife whom he had left at home with their two children. Too, letter writing was just not exactly his "thing". I have filled in the blanks that he has left with words of my own as I gleaned from books and diaries and museums. My photography, I hope, tells us some of McDonald's story in a visual way, as it comes out of my camera and my darkroom.

Though this publication is family oriented, and its purpose to instill interest and pride in his heirs who have inherited a history that is priceless, it is hoped it will be of value to others who live along this trail or had an ancestor who traveled it. For me it has been a fascinating time, looking for and photographing his Trail and relating his story in this little book.

There are some family members, who have contributed to my joy of producing this book, and I must thank them for their enthusiasm and encouragement. Dr. Edwin MacDonald Stanton [dec.], Schenectady, N. Y., senior grandson of James and Mary McDonald, who put his thought and effort into the original booklet of McDonald letters and who planted the "seed" in my mind, resulting in this publication. Mary Jean [Stoddard] Fowler, Houston, Texas, great granddaughter of James and Mary, for copies of the original hand written McDonald letters, and for family fotos and the art work at the bottom of these pages, and for review and comment of this work. Mary Margaret Stanton [dec.], my sister, for the use of her library. Staci Stanton, Mesa, Arizona, my granddaughter, for the art work on the cover. Douglas E. Stanton, my son, Live Oak, California, for review and comment of this work. Arthur H. Pickford, Jr., Dunlap, Illinois, great grandson of James and Mary, for family fotos. Virginia L. Stanton, my wonderful wife and companion, who helped me to put this project together.

Edgar W. Stanton, III
11476 Larkin Road
Live Oak, Calif. 95953

To My Father

JAMES McDONALD at Ames, Iowa about 1899

PREFACE to TREK OF JAMES McDONALD, 1850

The discovery of gold on the American River at Coloma in California by James Marshall in January, 1848, stirred the minds of most Americans. It was the promise of abundant riches described in reports [some true, but most exaggerated] trickling back to "The States" that excited the imagination of thousands of people, and so began the "Gold Rush" to California. People from all walks of life abandoned their way and joined the "stampede" westward.

James McDonald, the subject of this treatise, was one of those people [along with some 55,000 others] who in 1850 could not resist that lure of riches lying in the creeks and rivers of California. A cabinet maker by trade, he laid down his tools and joined that "Gold Rush".

The Missouri River, in the period 1849 and 1850, marked the boundary of Eastern America. Westward, beyond this wide river lay the Great Plains and the Great American Desert and the Rocky Mountains and the Sierra Nevadas -- this territory being mostly a mystery to the sojourners. Along the Missouri were several towns, mainly Independence, Fort Levenworth, St. Joseph and Council Bluffs, all at the beginning of "Emigrant Trails". these towns were the principal supply points where the emigrants could "fit out" their needs before departure -- horses, mules, oxen, wagons, rope, corn, pickles, flour, salt pork, coffee, tools, molasses, guns, powder, rice, lead, tents, medicines, stoves, cooking utensils, knives, canvas, lanterns, dried beef, sugar, sea biscuit, crackers, meat biscuit, beans, dried fruits, wagon axle grease, buckets, picks, shovels, playing cards, gunny sacks and whatever.

The McDonald company, consisting of a total of 4 men, chose St.

Joseph as their point of trail embarkation, arriving there about April 28, 1850, from New Concord, Ohio -- probably overland to an Ohio River port, and from there by river boat down the Ohio River and up the Mississippi River [Kentucky and Illinois and Wheeling and Cincinnati and St. Louis are mentioned] to St. Louis and then up the Missouri River to St. Joseph, about a 15 day trip. There they joined the tent city surrounding St. Joseph and commenced their preparations for their long two thousand mile journey west.

The outfitting period of this small group consumed two weeks. They along with hundreds of other excited travelers, moved about St. Joseph and neighboring towns searching for stock and whatever supplies needed for their venture west. The standard for transportation consisted of 1 wagon, 4 men, 6 oxen or mules (horses were not a popular draft stock) and 2000 pounds of supplies. As they accumulated materials for this journey a continual guard was necessary to protect against thieves, for this tent city had its share of scoundrels and roughnecks and schemers.

One of the most important decisions to be made was choice of stock for pulling the wagon -- mules or oxen? The prevailing opinion of the many who had started west and then decided to return was that oxen were the safest because of ease of handling by the inexperienced. They could live on feed that mules and horses wouldn't touch and were not so much a target for theft by the "friendly Indians". McDonald and company purchased 5 yoke of oxen and 2 ponies. Aware that on the Kansas side of the Missouri there were some 10,000 emigrants encamped awaiting the arrival of spring feed to show on the prairie, McDonald purchased a supply of corn to feed the stock for a few days in order to get on the road a bit ahead of the big flow of emigrants. **"The season is backward which throws us late of starting and the grass will not be as good as if the season had been early and the number going may make it scarce"** [Let.1, p.1].

There were some well organized groups of emigrants that had formed rather large companies to travel together. Larger organizations allowed for greater protection of its participants. These companies were made up of people whose skills could be utilized in cases of emergencies. There was need for the blacksmiths and carpenters and gunsmiths and mule skinners and cooks and hunters and doctors and ministers etc. Some wagons carried their specialties. There were the food wagons and repair wagons and mining supply wagons and "whatever" supply wagons. The greatest need for banding together was for protection from the Indians, so they imagined. Companies of 50 men and large numbers of wagons and stock were not uncommon.

McDonald and companions were only a "1 wagon outfit". It was common for some small units to buy their way into the larger companies. McDonald chose to keep small and perhaps join up with another wagon or two along the road. Throughout his journey he is on a first name basis with others than those members in his company. It must be presumed that he and two or three other "loners" have joined up sometime along the Trail. **"We have been in company for a week past with a man by the name of Cleveland of Missouri Sta. and perhaps will keep with him if we like his company and he ours"** [Let.2, p.1].

The McDonald Trail is the same Oregon-California Trail upon which thousands of gold seekers have emblazoned upon the ground and in letters and diaries a historical route from the Missouri River to California. Though McDonald did not digress so much in his correspondence to the family at home in New Concord, Ohio regarding the discomforts of the Trail, his company endured all the dangers and hardships of this Oregon-California route--the accidents, storms, sickness, stampedes, heat, cold, fatigue, dust, Indians. The energies required of all, in their daily tasks, were supreme just to stay alive and keep moving.

KEY TO PHOTO PAGES.

Foto 0   Oxen
1   Missouri River above St. Joseph
2   Presbyterian Mission
3   Big Blue River
4   Junction of The Ways
5   Fort Kearney
6   Six Miles West, encamped
7   45 miles above Ft. Kearney
8   South Fork, 23 miles above
9   3 miles to the North Fork
10   Ash Hollow
11   View from Kelley grave.
12   North Platte Valley from North side
13   Courthouse Rock
14   Chimney Rock
15   Castle Rock
16   Scott's Bluff
17   Wagon at Scott's Bluff
18   Robidoux Blacksmith Shop
19   Unmarked graves and Robidoux Pass
20   North Platte Bottom
21   Fort Laramie
22   8 miles west of Ft. Laramie
23   Gurnsey wagon ruts
24   Crossing North Platte at Casper
25   EWS and Oregon Trail marker
26   1986 Oregon Trail travelers
27   Willow Springs
28   Sweetwater River to east
29   Sweetwater River to west
30   Independence Rock
31   Devils Gate [on Sun Ranch]
32   Wind blown section of Trail
33   Sweetwater River and Trail
34   Split Rock
35   Sweetwater River Valley
36   11 miles from South Pass
37   South Pass
38   Pacific Springs
39   Rocky Mountains
40   Plume Rock
41   Dry Sandy
42   Sublette Cutoff forks
43   Little Sandy River
44   Big Sandy River
45   Green River
46   Ham's Fork of Green River
47   Sublette at Smith's Fork
48   Bear River

KEY TO FOTO PAGES

Introduction to Photographic Section

The following pages are made up of excerpts from the McDonald letters and a related photograph of the place or thing mentioned. Each page also has some bit of dissertation regarding the photo and the occasion.

That portion of the trail from Soda Springs, Idaho to Lovelock, Nevada [July 22 to August 23] McDonald has left for other 1850 travelers to inform us with their diaries and letters.

Two character sizes have been used to differentiate between McDonald letter excerpts and "filler" from other sources. Larger characters [10 characters per inch] mark the McDonald source and the smaller characters [12 characters per inch] mark other sources. The bibliography of "other sources" is found at the end of this book.

There are four map pages showing portions of 7 states. On these map pages are numbers and site locations of 72 photographs and a stippled line drawn from St.Joseph, Missouri to Sacramento City, California. This line marks the trail of James McDonald and 1,950 "wagon traveled" miles of his participation in a most historical event in the life of America.

There is a story, "THE TREK", accompanying the following map and "Foto" pages in which James McDonald had some part in the writing. This story helps us to better know his trials and trail. His words are in **bold type with quotation marks** and referenced.

The photographs taken in the field, while looking for great grandfather McDonald's footprints, and the dark room work to produce these pictures was done by Edgar W. Stanton, III.

The word "recruit" has been challenged by reviewers and thus needs some clarification. It is used by diarists of 1850 era and is defined in Webster's New World Dictionary and Webster's Collegiate Dictionary as: [Rare] a) to increase or maintain by supplying anew; replenish. b) to revive or restore health. c) to provide with what is needed to correct or prevent exhaustion. d) To restore vigor.

Foto No. 0.   HORNS DO NOT AN OXEN MAKE.

St. Joseph, Mo. May 12, 1850

Dear Mary:

It is now nine o'clock at night. I am writing on our table by the side of our tent. It is my turn to watch the cattle. It is necessary to keep a guard as there is a great deal of stealing done in this place............We have bought 4 yoke of cattle - very good ones, for which we paid $300. We will buy another yoke in the morning...........We will start sometime in the day to try the traveling. We are camping now two weeks.............

MAY 1850

S	M	T	W	T	F	S
			1	2	3	4
5	6	7	8	9	10	11
12	13	14	15	16	17	18
19	20	21	22	23	24	25
26	27	28	29	30	31	

The frontier river town of St. Joseph, Missouri, is the beginning of the McDonald Trail. Founded by Joseph Robidoux in 1826. Called Blacksnake Hills and renamed St. Joseph in 1843. At the height of the emigration, this little town was swarming with many travelers from all walks of life including the riffraff of camp followers -gamblers, robbers, thieves, murderers and schemers of every kind.

15

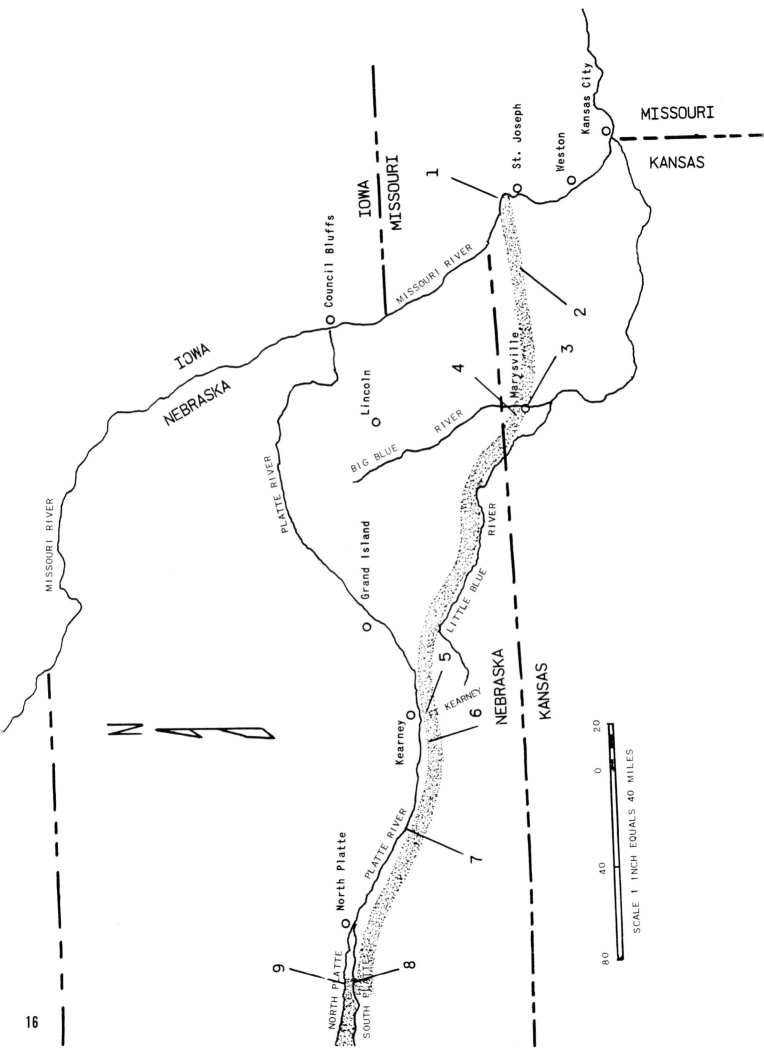

MISSOURI

KANSAS

Kansas City

Weston

St. Joseph

MISSOURI

IOWA

1

2

Council Bluffs

MISSOURI RIVER

3

Marysville

4

IOWA

NEBRASKA

Lincoln

BIG BLUE RIVER

PLATTE RIVER

MISSOURI RIVER

Grand Island

LITTLE BLUE RIVER

5

KANSAS

NEBRASKA

FT. KEARNEY

6

Kearney

N

7

PLATTE RIVER

North Platte

9

NORTH PLATTE

SOUTH PLATTE

8

SCALE 1 INCH EQUALS 40 MILES

20 0 40 80

16

SCALE of DISTANCES from St. JOSEPH

```
                                                Miles
St.  Joseph,  Mo........................................0
Missouri River Crossing.....................5
The Agency,  Kn.............................35
Marysville,  Kn.............................99
Junction of ways,  Kn......................108
Kansas-Nebraska Boundary...................129
Ft.  Kearney,  Nebr.........................256
23 mi.  above the Forks....................370
3 mi.  to North Fork.......................373
Ash Hollow.................................422
Chimney Rock...............................493
Platte Bottom,  Nebr.......................534
Ft.  Laramie,  Wyo..........................569
Casper,  North Platte Crossing.............669
Independence Rock,  Wyo....................724
South Pass,  Continental divide............824
Green River................................892
Cokeville,  Wyo.  Smith's Fork.............948
Soda Springs,  Idaho......................1006
Fort Hall.................................1056
Raft River,  Turnoff on Calif Trail......1103
City Of Rocks.............................1145
Idaho-Nevada Boundary.....................1166
Elko,  Nevada.............................1292
Winnemucca................................1426
Rye Patch.................................1460
Lovelock,  "18 miles above the Sink"......1497
Ragtown...................................1552
Nevada-California Boundary................1626
Hangtown..................................1682
Sacramento City...........................1723
```

These are map scaled distances and must be multiplied by factor of 1.13 for a more realistic "wagon traveled" miles.

THE TREK

On Monday, May 13, 1850 the group, -- being **James McDonald**, Ben Metcalf, Dr. Hugh Parks, and Isaac Walters -- departed St. Joseph, Missouri, traveled up the river 5 miles, encamped, ferried across to the Kansas side in early morning of May 14, and began their great Trek to California. McDonald and company head west on a rather circuitous road through a heavily wooded country for about 27 miles to an Indian made and owned toll bridge across Wolf Creek, 25¢ to 50¢ to cross. McDonald made no comment. He either paid or forded. Most travelers paid just to save time and trouble. At thirty miles from St. Joseph he came to the "INDIAN AGENCY" and Presbyterian Mission (one and the same?).

Some wagons on the St. Joseph branch that have been loaded too heavily are having trouble getting along with much progress because of bogging in the "heavy" and wet soil. These drivers are having to lighten loads by discarding some of their burden. This debris, showing along the roadside so soon after leaving St. Joseph, is only the beginning sign of problems. Sickness, the dreaded Asian cholera, has begun to show its mark by the numbers of graves seen along the way and at the banks of the Big Blue River. The St. Joseph branch of the Oregon Trail crossed the Big Blue River at present day Marysville, Kansas and joined with the Independence branch 8 miles west and 2 miles north from this Big Blue crossing. As the McDonald wagon and company follow the Trail westerly along the ridge of the hill from the Big Blue crossing, they look to their left at the white tops of the multitude of covered wagons on the Independence branch and the great cloud of dust they create, and behind them, on the St. Joseph road is the same dusty scene. Ahead of them a short distance the trails meet. Beyond the junction is seen an unending stream of emigrant trains and their ever-cursed dust. Today, from the trail junction marker, walk east up the hill to

the crest and there see McDonald footsteps in a beautifully farmed cornfield. These footsteps are, by McDonald count, about 119 trail miles from St."Jo".

McDonald, now on the full Oregon-California Trail, travels northwesterly 25 miles to the little Blue River and continues on that course along the Little Blue until it turns southerly. He moves on northwesterly to the Platte River and thence along the south bank of the Platte to Fort Kearney, arriving there without incident on May 30, 1850, distant 282 miles from St. Joseph. **"We have had no accidents or trouble"** [Let.2, p.1]. Spirits appear high with McDonald and company. Their health is good. Sighting of the numerous graves (last year's and this year's) does not seem to bother them. Road conditions have been excellent, except for a few stream crossings. Buffalo and antelope have been sighted. They have been on the open prairie since arriving at the Little Blue. **"Grass is plenty......If the journey is no harder than we have seen, it is nothing"** [Let.3, p.1]. At this point on the Trail, "seeing the elephant", so often referred to as that moment of total discouragement whereupon a man gives up and turns about in the trail and "heads for home", appears a total myth to this little group. Fort Laramie is 344 miles ahead.

McDonald passes Fort Kearney on May 30 and **"encamped 6 miles west.......There are** (at Fort Kearney) **two or three frame houses, the balance are made of sod cut into square blocks and built like stone"** [Let.3, p.1]. Fort Kearney was important to McDonald only for mailing his Letter No. 2 and for passing this milestone of the journey. For most of the emigrants, however, stopping at Fort Kearney was a respite from the toils of the trail. There were repairs to be made and articles to purchase at the Sutler's store and inquiries regarding the road ahead and of people that have passed and more lightening of loads, and always the need for assistance. One thousand wagons passed Fort Kearney each day. That means the result of 4000 people driving some 8000 head of

stock pouring in on such a small military development was overwhelming. To commemorate this place, there is a National Monument office and museum, some well kept wagons to view and a replica of a blacksmith shop. The trees planted by the soldiers have since grown into large trees.

McDonald continues westward along the south side of the Platte River. He is on the Great Plains. **"There is no timber of any note. On the islands in the Platte there is some cottonwood and willows but of an inferior quality. For the first 200 miles up the Platte there is but little variation of scenery. The river is from ½ to 1 mile wide studded thick with small islands"** [Let.3, p.1]. This is monotonous traveling, mile after mile of sameness--heat, dust, enforced companionship, fatigue, balky and lame animals, Cholera and smallpox, and for some unfortunates, death and burials. This all is beginning to wear on the souls of men, and the journey is hardly under way. Not all burials are due to sickness. Accidents and drownings have taken a toll. All emigrants armed themselves for that fight with the Indians that never came about. Many of these men were incompetent with their gun handling. There were those whose morality was questionable from the start, and the decay in some of the souls of these individuals appeared in robbery and murder.

The emigrants continue in the process of lightening their loads. One of the first items to be tossed out were stoves. On entering the plains there was no wood to burn. Stoves were now a useless burden. This little company does not mention its "load lightening" order. If they had a stove, it would be gone by now. McDonald apparently was the cook. He, along with all other cooks on the trail, had to burn that famous fuel the "buffalo chip". When stopping at the end of the day there was always a mad scramble of the cooks out gathering and competing for dry chips.

Continued on p. 31

Foto No. 1.   THE WIDE MISSOURI, upstream from ST. JOSEPH.

........We left St. Joseph, as I stated in my last [letter], on the 13th about 4 o'clock in the evening. We went up the river 5 miles and crossed in the morning early.......

Long lines of teams and wagons and loose stock, with their cursing drivers and herders jockying and fighting for a position in line to board the ferries, jammed the streets of St. Joseph. The view of this disarray of animals, equipment and men must have suggested to McDonald and Company that there were better ferry locations and thus chose to travel upstream 5 miles to a more suitable ferry site.

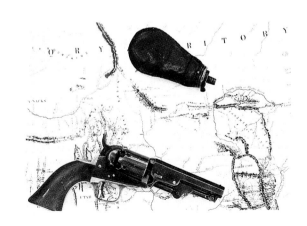

This 1849 COLT Pocket Pistol and "Powder Horn" make a good pair for a Trail Companion.

Foto No. 2.   PRESBYTERIAN MISSIONARY STATION

..........we passed an Indian encampment - the first we have seen since we passed a place called the Agency, 30 miles from St. Joseph.............

McDonald must have possessed one of the guide books available at St. Louis stores, containing a description of important landmarks and water courses he would encounter and a table of distances from point to point. The INDIAN AGENCY mentioned by McDonald, and the Presbyterian Mission mentioned by others are listed in Street's guide book as being 30 miles from St. Joseph, and in close proximity to each.

Foto No. 3.   BIG BLUE RIVER, KANSAS

At 122 miles west of St. Joseph, the trail crossed the Big Blue River at the present town of Marysville, Kansas. When this river was high, due to the storms, it was necessary to float the wagon boxes across with their gear aboard or wait for the water to subside and ford the stream. Some comments by emigrants: wood is plenty - river high, building a raft - river is low, fording good - many big catfish - large city of tents - game of all kinds, elk, deer, antelope - soil rich - old graves, fresh graves. McDonald would have crossed the Big Blue River near this point on about May 20, 1850.

Foto No. 4.   JUNCTION of INDEPENDENCE ROAD and St. JOSEPH ROAD.

This marker is located 8 miles west and 2 miles north of the town of Marysville, Kansas, and fixes the location of the joining of the Overland Trail [from St. Joseph] and the Oregon Trail [from Independence], referred to as "Junction of the Ways". St. Joseph museum information and a local farm resident place this intersection at about 120 rods NORTHWEST from this marker. Walk east along a farm road up a gentle slope about 60 rods and stand on the ridge of the hill along which is the St. Joseph road and there, perhaps, are McDonald footsteps in a beautifuly farmed corn field [in 1986].

Emigrants, as they approach this junction on the St. Joseph trail, observe the long lines of white covered wagons behind them and to their left on the Independence road and beyond the joining of the roads - an unending stream of emigrant trains and their ever-cursed dust.

MULES were the makings of many fine teams.

Foto No. 5.   FORT KEARNEY, NEBRASKA.

Platte Bottom, June 13, 1850

Dear Mary:

.................As I wrote from Ft. Kearney I will commence there. We passed it on the 30th of May [Thursday], encamped six miles west. There are two or three frame houses, the balance are made of sod cut into square blocks and built like stone.........

Fort Kearney is located 1 mile south of the Platte River near the upstream end of Grand Island. In 1850 there were no fortifications or walls - only an encampment of soldiers. The "sod" building in the foto houses the blacksmith shop [in 1986].

......If you see a spot, you conclude it is an animal and name it by its size and color. We have seen some buffalo and several antelopes. Some of the companies have killed both kinds.........

Foto No. 6. PLATTE RIVER

........We passed it [Ft. Kearney] on the 30th of May --
encamped 6 miles west..........

............There is no timber of any note. On the islands in
the Platte there is some cottonwood and willows but of an
inferior quality. For the first 200 miles up the Platte, there
is but little variation of scenery. The river is from ½ to 1
mile wide, studded thick with small islands............

Emigrant comment: "A mile wide and an inch deep".

This foto of the Platte River is about 6 miles upstream from Ft. Kearney and
is from the Mormon side and looking to the West. Timber now line the banks
of this great river. McDonald, apparently, did not stop for long at Ft.
Kearney [only to deposit letter No. 2 ?] and chose to proceed to a camping
area in this vicinity.

Foto No. 7.   PLATTE RIVER 45 miles from the Fort [Kearney]

..........We laid by on Sunday [June 2, 1850] about 45 miles from the Fort [Kearney]. In the afternoon we heard there was a man by the name of Clapp encamped on the other side on the Mormon road leading from Council Bluffs. Metcalf and I swam over to see him but it was not the man we wanted. The river is from six inches to 6 feet deep, the bottom quicksands, the water runs rapid and muddy - boiling like the Missouri..............

"Too thick to drink and too thin to plow".

Foto is of the PLATTE RIVER at about 45 miles upstream from Fort Kearney, Nebraska taken from the Mormon side.

Foto No. 8.   SOUTH FORK OF THE PLATTE RIVER, 23 miles above the forks.

..........We forded the South Fork of [the] Platte River about 4 o'clock the 5 th of June. The water was from 1 to $2\frac{1}{2}$ ft. deep, the bottom quicksands. We could not let the cattle stop as the sand would settle away and our wagon go down. The river is from $\frac{1}{4}$ to $\frac{1}{2}$ mile wide. This crossing is about 23 miles above the forks of the river [Platte].........

JUNE 1850

S	M	T	W	T	F	S
						1
2	3	4	5	6	7	8
9	10	11	12	13	14	15
16	17	18	19	20	21	22
23 30	24	25	26	27	28	29

Foto No. 8 is at a point 23 miles above the forks of the Platte River. Camera stands on the south bank of the south fork. Rock riprap controls river bank erosion. This foto - September 1986.

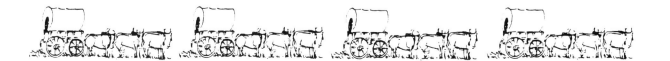

Foto No. 9.   NORTH FORK OF THE PLATTE RIVER, 23 miles above the forks.

..........We crossed over the bluffs, [traveling] about 3 miles to the North Fork.........

Foto from the south bank of the North Platte River, September 1987, 23 miles above the forks. Here McDonald and company turned toward the west [away from camera] and followed along the south bank - this on June 5 late [Wednesday], or June 6 early [Thursday].

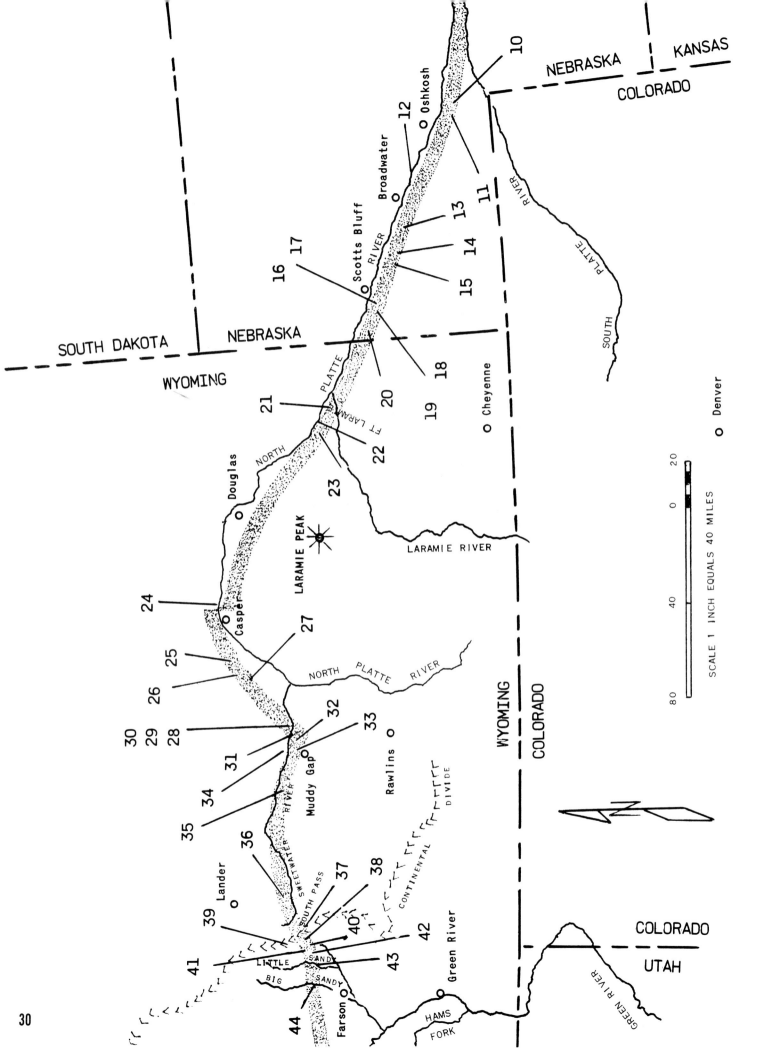

30

From p. 20

One hundred twenty five miles from Ft. Kearney, McDonald passes the forks of the Platte, and now continues upstream along the south side of the South Platte River for 23 miles. **"We forded the south fork of the Platte about 4 o'clock the 5th of June. The water was from 1 to 2½ ft. deep, the bottom quick sands, We could not let the cattle stop as the sand would settle away and our wagon go down........This crossing is about 23 miles above the forks of the river"** [Let.3, p.1]. He then travels north, over the bluffs, about 3 miles to the north fork of the Platte, and then upstream (west), along the south side of the North Fork of the Platte River.

This is buffalo country and every "hunter" on the trail is looking for his chance to score a hit. Of all buffalo killed, only a relatively few were eaten. Though it was good meat and fresh and many emigrants feasted, the sport of the hunt resulted in a major overkill. It was the beginning of the demise of the buffalo herds--the staple food of the Indian. This is Indian country. The Indians are encamped along the river and the Emigrant Trail and remain in this country so long as the buffalo remain. When the herds migrate northward the Indians follow. By late June the buffalo and Indians are gone from the North Platte River Valley. McDonald and company are witness to the Indian encampments and the Indian migration. **"June 12th passed another Indian encampment. They were pulling up stakes to move......The Chiefs have briefs from the officers of the forts stating the friendship and good behavior of the Chiefs and asking a little bread, sugar, coffee, flour, etc. as a compensation for the whites driving the buffalo from the river"** [Let.3, p.1 & 2].

"The health of the emigration is quite different from what it was when I last wrote. Since we have been on this river, sickness has been increasing, principally diarrhea. Some die very suddenly with it" [Let.3, p.2]. Cholera is now the scourge of

this Oregon-California Trail. It is the leading killer of the emigrants. A man could eat a hearty breakfast and be buried at noon. A quick but agonizing death awaited many. This sickness was so frightening that it caused companions to lose their sense of reasoning. Burials of the dead (and some not so dead) were made in hastily dug graves at minimum depths. By morning following burial, wolves would have dug up the remains and eaten their fill. Some burials were made in the trail to keep the wolves from finding the bodies. On occasion the sick were left by their companions beside the trail to die on someone else's sympathies. One diarist reports giving one of these unfortunates a cup of water. The next day he recovered. Someone in California has a surprise coming. **"This diarrhea cuts them off sometimes in a few hours, but we will try to meet it promptly and trust to God for consequences"** [Let.3, p.3].

The source and transmission of cholera was unknown to the emigrants. This disease was intestinal in its source and was spread by drinking water contaminated by human filth. Also the dust of the trail is thought to spread the disease as human and animal feces were ground in with the dust and inhaled by the travelers. Emigrants gave no thought to and saw no need for sanitation. Garbage and offal were left behind as people encamped and then moved on. This rotting environment was a contribution from all emigrants to their own ill health.

The scene along the Platte has changed but little along the way from Ft. Kearney -- Buffalo, antelope, prickly pear, prairie dogs, Indians, dust, offal, mules, horses, oxen, graves, cursing drivers, wagons, discarded posessions. **"what can be said of one mile can be said of it all"** [Let.3, p.1]. A spring issuing from a hollow in the low hills at ASH HOLLOW breaks the monotony with a bit of fresh water. The emigrants continue on the Trail on the south side of the North Platte and eventually arrive at some **"splendid scenery, landscapes, Courthouse Rock, Chimney Rock,**

Castle Bluff (Rock), Scotts Bluff" [Let.3, p.2]. Chimney Rock shows up like a great majestic spire, and if the air is clear, can be seen for 25 or 30 miles. McDonald passes this landmark on about June 12, 1850 after traveling some 557 miles from St. Joseph. Traveling up the Platte Valley, McDonald and company are averaging 24+ miles per day of travel, which indicates they are pushing their teams. They are, however, equipped with two extra yoke of oxen which allows them to rotate their draft animals.

"We passed another Indian village today (June 13, 1850). There are some white men among them. One has a blacksmith shop. We get the use of it to make some ox shoes and nails" [Let.3, p.2]. Antoine Robidoux owned a trading post and blacksmith shop located on the Trail about 8 miles west southwest of Scotts Bluff. Rental of the blacksmith shop to the emigrants was 75¢ per hour. This was a very popular place and mentioned by most diarists.

"This is now Saturday, the 15th (of June, 1850), 8 miles west of Ft. Laramie. We have encamped for the purpose of staying until Monday. We passed the fort at 12 o'clock. We had to drive out here to get pasture and will take our letters back to the Fort" [Let.3, p.3]. Fort Laramie, lying between the forks of the North Platte and the Laramie Rivers, was an eagerly anticipated stop along this Oregon-California Trail. Stopping here gave all a break in the labors of travel. McDonald and company have covered "....from St. Joseph....641 miles...." [Let.3, p.2]. They are one of the "...1000...wagons passed the fort...today" [Let.3, p.3]. In 1850, The fort consisted of an encampment of soldiers. Old Bedlam (a bachelor officers quarters) and the Sutler's store, both built in 1849, have since been reconditioned and are a part of the Fort Laramie National Monument. We searched for historical record of James McDonald in the Fort archives and found nothing. The original registry is reported lost(in 1987).

From Fort Laramie to the Mormon Ferry Crossing on the North

Platte (near Casper, Wyoming), the road goes through the Black Hills. **"The road was hard and sharp on the cattle's feet. Their feet were worn to the quick and hindered their traveling some."** [Let.4, p.1]. This 110 miles of trail received universal complaint from the emigrants.

The North Platte in this vicinity can not be forded, the river being too deep and current too strong. The McDonald company chooses to use a ferry 3 miles below the Mormon Ferry because informers have told them it would be a 10 day wait before their turn to cross. **"We therefore bargained for $5 to take our wagon and load over, which was done by 1 o'clock."** (June 21, 1850) [Let.4, p.1]. The North Platte in this area was the death of many emigrants. At this crossing, of the many ferry crossings, 5 men were drowned June 21, 1850. **"We drove three miles Sunday morning** (June 23) **to pasture at the Upper Ferry"** (Mormon Ferry)   [Let.4, p.1].

The Great Plains are now passed. On the north bank of the North Platte the Mormon Trail and the Oregon-California trail join. This is now the beginning of the Great American Desert, and from here on to the west McDonald and company are faced with a barren land over which they must travel. This is sage brush and alkali country. Good water and feed are hardly to be found for the next 52 miles to the Sweetwater River. Most of the pools of water found on this trail section are poisoned with alkali, and thirst crazed animals are difficult to control and keep from these poison pools. Many emigrants were unable to hold their stock back from heading for this deadly water as evidenced by the dead and rotting animals ringing the pools and strung out along the trail. A head count runs high of oxen, few mules or horses.

At 27 miles from the Platte crossing McDonald comes· to WILLOW SPRINGS, a refreshing place in this desert. Water here is good but feed sparse. This is a favorable place for the emigrants to

Continued on p. 54

34

Plat t Bottom June 13   1850

Dear Mary as this is my Watch night I
thaught I would Ocipy a part of it in writing to you
the Boys all talks of writing from Ft Laramy and we doo
not expect to stop long there and our time ware when laying
By is in a good part taken up in tending to the cattle and Horses
I thaught I would Ocipy this Lonely hour it is raining a little
and I am setting in the wagon the wind shakes it a mast to
Bad to write as I wrote from Ft karney I will commence
there we pased it on the 30th of may Eaconpt 6 miles west
there is two or three frame houses the Balance are made of
Sod cut into Square Blocks and Built like stone there is
no timber of any note on the Islands in the Plat there
is some cotton wood and willows But of an inferiour quality
for the first 2 hundred miles up the plat there is But little
variation of sceenery the river is from ½ to 1 mile wide
studed thick with small Islands we laid By on sunday
about 45 miles from the ft in the afternoon we heard
there was a Man By the name of Clap incompt on the other
side on the Mormon road Leading from council Bluffs
Metcalf and I swam over to see him But it was not
the man we wanted the River is from six inches to 6 ft
Deep the Bottom quick sands the water runs Rapid and
Muddy Boiling like the Mosurie we forded the south fork
of plat about 4 oc the fifth of June the water was from
1 to 2½ ft deep the Bottom quick sands we could not let the
cattle stop as the sand would settle away and our wagon go down
the river is from ¼ to ½ mile wide this crossing is about
23 miles above the forks of the River we crosed over the Bluffs
about 3 miles to the North fork Sunday June 9th Laid
By from 1 oc we left in the morning on account of Bad pasture
June 10th too Day we pased an indian incamptment the first

Foto No. 10.   ASH HOLLOW, Nebraska.

................We saw "Calvin P. McDonald of Concord June 5, 1850" on a tree in Ash Hollow. We passed it on the 8th [of June]............

This foto is of the mouth of Ash Hollow. The McDonald trail passes from right to left, paralleling the county road. North Platte River is seen approximately ½ mile beyond the road. At base of the far hill on the left is a cemetery with pioneer graves. The "California Hill" segment of the Oregon Trail entered Ash Hollow about 3 miles south of camera and both trails meet near the cemetery. Camera looks to northwest.

To communicate with those friends or relatives following on the trail, the emigrants resorted to many means such as leaving notes attached to walls of trading posts or left in barrels marked "Post Office" or on signs attached to trees or painted on rocks. Some left their marks on buffalo skulls beside the trail.

Foto No. 11. NORTH PLATTE RIVER NEAR ASH HOLLOW.

On June 8, 1850 McDonald and his team passed right to left [going west] through this hay field between camera and North Platte River. Oregon Trail marker and Kelly grave are behind camera. This site is 1½ miles west of mouth of Ash Hollow.

Of the thousands who died on this Oregon-California Trail there are but a few whose name marks their grave.

A man's name is his nearest and dearest posession and the only thing "he takes with him".

Foto No. 12. NORTH PLATTE RIVER

.........June 10 we passed an Indian encampment - the first we have seen since we passed a place called The Agency 30 miles from St. Joseph. The scenery on the Platte so far is much of a sameness. What can be said of one mile can be said of it all - bluffs on one side, the river on the other. The bottom is from 5 to 8 miles wide [with] no timber except, as I said, on the islands and occasionally a small red cedar in the hollows of the bluffs.........

Foto taken from a bluff on the north [Mormon] side of the North Platte River overlooking the North Platte Bottom. McDonald traveled from left to right [west] on the flat land beyond the river. Prorating time and distance places him in this Foto on June 10, 1850 between present day Lisco and Broadwater, Nebraska. The Indians, too, have passed.

Foto No. 13. COURTHOUSE ROCK and JAIL ROCK.

..............yesterday we passed by some splendid scenery, landscapes - COURTHOUSE ROCK..........

Prorating time and distance westward from Ash Hollow and eastward from Fort Laramie, McDonald would have passed Courthouse Rock and Chimney Rock on June 11, 1850 and Castle Bluff [Rock] and Scotts Bluff on June 12, 1850.

Foto 14. CHIMNEY ROCK

...............Chimney Rock...........

To the travelers of 1849-1850 Chimney Rock excelled as a guide and landmark. Rising up out of the North Platte River valley it could be seen for some 30 miles distant and was a most welcome sight to the emigrants. Emigrant guide books had alerted these travelers to this exceptional mark and kept every one looking with anticipation for their first sighting. Today [1986] the spire stands as a monument to those sturdy pioneers, though it be some worn down by time and the elements.

Many names were carved in the sandstone bluffs along the trail. There are but few names that have survived the wear of these 136 years. S. H. Patrick June 6, 1850. Register Cliff at Guernsey, Wyoming.

Foto No. 15. CASTLE BLUFF [ROCK]

..........Castle Bluff.........

McDonald is one of the few who mention this "Rock" that also marks the way for the emigrants. It stands large and prominent above the North Platte River Valley, approximately 13 miles before Scotts Bluff.

THIS KETTLE CAME ACROSS THE PLAINS.

Foto No. 16.   SCOTTS BLUFF

.........Scotts Bluff, etc. These I would describe but I have not room..........

Today, Scotts Bluff is recognized for its historical value by its place in the National Monument system. This is another of those scenic wonders found along the western part of the North Platte valley in Nebraska and mentioned by most diarists. McDonald says but little regarding the scenery along his trail. His thoughts and energies appear to be spent in the toil of moving ever westward.

PRAIRIE DOG

Foto No. 17.   COVERED WAGON, Scotts Bluff National Monument.

........It is frequently remarked by men as we pass, "There is a team and wagon that will go through"........

This wagon is the typical prairie schooner of the Plains. It stands at the Scotts Bluff National Monument, Nebraska. Most of these wagons were the common farm vehicle used for heavy work. The bed was about 10 feet long and 4 feet wide with sides two or three feet high and topped by five or six bows of hickory upon which was stretched a heavy canvas covering waterproofed by a boiling mixture of linseed oil and bee's wax. Three yoke of oxen could pull this wagon loaded with 2000 pounds of weight. McDonald and Company must have made a wise purchase as their wagon was saleable after surviving 1750 miles [to the Carson River, Nevada].

Foto No. 18   VIRGINIA STANTON AT SITE OF ROBIDOUX BLACKSMITH SHOP

..............We passed another Indian village today. There were some white men among them. One has a blacksmith shop. We get the use of it to make some ox shoes and nails. Hugh and Jim stopped and we drove on. Hugh caught up at noon, but Jim stopped to cut and weld the tire of a wagon for George Wilson..........

Antoine Robidoux was the proprietor of a trading post and blacksmith shop housed in a log shack located about 8 miles west southwest of Scotts Bluff, Nebraska. He lived with his Indian wife and family in an Indian Lodge. Robidoux rented out his tools and shop to the emigrants for 75¢ per hour. He, being a trader, dealt with many an emigrant for some of their posessions for which he paid but little [a wagon for 75¢]. McDonald stopped here on June 13, 1850.

OX SHOES.

Foto No. 19.   UNNAMED GRAVES AT ROBIDOUX PASS, Nebraska.

...........The health of the emigration is quite different now from what it was when I last wrote [from Ft. Kearney]. Since we have been on this river sickness has been increasing, principally diarrhea. Some die very suddenly with it. It is by some called the cholera, but we think not. I suppose it is occasioned by drinking the water of this vicinity........

McDonald has said very little regarding the sickness that befell most all the emigrants. Only through the activities of Dr. Parks is there a hint as to the extent of the sickness troubles on the Trail. Cholera was the scourge of this movement. The source and spread of this disease was unknown to the emigrants, and as a result there were no precautions taken. Contamination of nearly every drinkable water source lead to its spread. The sluggish and muddy Platte River contributed its share to the problem. The Cholera struck hard and fast. A man could eat a hearty breakfast and be buried at noon.

McDonald makes no mention of the numbers of deaths or graves observed in his daily travel. His silence in his letters on this subject was, no doubt, to keep from alarming his family at home in Ohio.

Accidents, Cholera, Smallpox, Scurvy and "Mountain Fever" accounted for the greatest number of deaths of the emigrants.

Foto No. 20.   NORTH PLATTE RIVER BOTTOM.

Platte Bottom, June 13, 1850

Dear Mary:

As this is my watch night I thought I would occupy a part of it in writing to you. The boys all talk of writing from Fort Laramie and we do not expect to stop long there and our time, even when laying by, is in a good part taken up in tending to the cattle and horses. I thought I would occupy this lonely hour. It is raining a little and I am sitting in the wagon. The wind shakes it almost too bad to write...........We are now about 35 or 40 miles from Ft. Laramie. We expect to get there day after tomorrow. We will then be out from St. Joseph five weeks and [will] have made a distance of 641 miles...........

June 13, 1850 places McDonald in the North Platte bottom near the Nebraska - Wyoming line. The line of trees marks the south bank of the North Platte River. This foto is of the bottom land adjacent the river and about 1 mile east of the Nebraska border. In 1850 there were no trees.

Foto No. 21. SUTLER'S STORE AT FORT LARAMIE.

.........We passed the Fort [Laramie] at 12 o'clock
[Saturday, June 15, 1850]..........They keep a register of names,
number of men, women, horses, mules, cattle, wagons, etc. we
there found the names of Mc's [another McDonald from New Concord,
Ohio?] boys, Cambridge boys, Evansburg boys and all we
wanted........I must now give you the the number that have gone
and had their names registered. There had passed on the 14th
[Friday, June 14, 1850] 23,292 men, 363 women, 375 children,
6,345 wagons, 18,436 horses, 5,955 mules, 14,072 oxen, 1,689
cows. How many have passed and not gone and had their names put
down we cannot guess. How many have gone the Mormon trail we
cannot even guess.......There were about 1200 wagons passed the
Fort last Thursday, 900 or 1000 today and the crowd thickest
behind us. It will continue but for a few days........

The foto is of the Sutler's store at Fort Laramie. That portion of the
building shown in the picture was built in 1849 and one of two buildings of
that era now standing. Did James McDonald pass through that portal? Standing
at the doorway is Edgar W. Stanton, III, a great grandson of James and Mary
McDonald.

Today, at Fort Laramie, there is no record of a registry with the name of
James McDonald on June 15, 16 or 17, 1850.

Foto No. 22.   NORTH PLATTE RIVER, 8 Miles west of Ft. Laramie.

..........This is now Saturday the 15th [of June], 8 miles west of Ft. Laramie. We have encamped for the purpose of staying until Monday [June 17].........We had to drive out here to get pasture and will take our letters back to the Fort [Laramie]...........Our pasture has been poor for the last 100 miles, yet we cannot perceive the cattle falling away much. Some of the heavy ones are getting their feet tender by wearing off..........while I have my health, I think the hardships and privations, at least what I have seen, as nothing worth mentioning although we see some almost every day going back discouraged...........

This is a view toward the upstream [west] of the North Platte River some 8 miles above Fort Laramie. McDonald encamped in this vicinity on the nights of June 15 and 16, 1850. Though he complains but little of the hardships, the wear and tear on the human mind and body and on the equipage of the emigrants is taking place. Mounting numbers of deaths, loss of stock, loss of provisions, breakage of wagons, sickness and fatigue have resulted in discouragement to some and a few of these people are returning to "the States".

Distance Ft. Kearney to Ft. Laramie equals 344 wagon traveled miles. McDonald covers this in 14¼ traveling days, averaging 24.2 miles per day. This is easy traveling up the Platte River valley. He does well.

Foto No. 23.   WAGON RUTS near Gurnsey, Wyoming.

..........As I expect, you have received a letter from me written from Ft. Kearney and one from Ft. Laramie. I will commence at that place [Ft. Laramie] but I will be brief. We left our encampment [8 miles west of Ft. Laramie] on Monday following [June 17, 1850], crossed the Black Hills. The road was hard and sharp on the cattle's feet. Their feet were worn to the quick and hindered their traveling some, yet we got along very well........

If McDonald's encampment was near the North Platte River, he would have traveled along the trail through the Platte bottom about 3 miles and perhaps climbed this hill. Many wagons plus the weather have left their mark. These ruts, cut in the sandstone, are near Gurnsey, Wyoming.

Foto below is of the Laramie Mountains with Laramie Peak [elevation 10,274 ft.] standing out as a distant and prominent landmark.

Foto No. 24.   NORTH PLATTE RIVER near Casper, Wyoming.

..........We got to the Ferry on the north branch of the Platte River on Friday [June 21] at 9 o'clock, 110 miles from the Laramie fort. There is a ferry 3 [text reads 30] miles above this place, but the emigrants rode forward to see what chance there was to cross. They returned and said there were so many they would not get across for ten days. We concluded to try it here altho their boats were very inferior...........We therefore bargained for $ 5 to take our wagon and load over which was done by 1 o'clock [Friday, June 21, 1850]...........We drove three miles [on] Sunday [June 23, 1850] morning to pasture at the Upper Ferry.........

McDonald and Company traveled across the Black Hills 102 miles in 4¼ days to a ferry site near Casper, Wyoming, averaging 24 miles per day.

John B. Hill on June 21, 1850 [same day as McDonald], bargained for $5.00 to have his wagon ferried across the North Platte River. Same site?

On this date [June 21, 1850] 5 men were drowned at this ferry site in crossing accidents.

Foto No. 25.   EMIGRANT TRAIL ROAD. Wyoming trail marker 15 miles southwest of Casper.

............Since we left the Platte River the
country has been barren and sandy..........

The above short sentence describes the next 52 miles of the McDonald trail.
The area along this stretch of the Oregon Trail has changed but little during
these past 136 years. It is a land for a few cattle and antelope.

Foto No. 26.   1986 OREGON TRAIL TRAVELERS.

We are encamped for the night right on the Oregon Trail, 6 miles before Willow Springs. Beyond the vehicle about half a mile is a spring making this area, no doubt, a place for encampments. One thousand wagons and teams passed through this scene with James McDonald and Company perhaps June 24, 1850, moving from right to left. This site is at about half the distance on the 52 mile stretch of trail between the North Platte River crossing and the Sweetwater River. Today, gone is the dust and refuse and turmoil created by those thousands of wagons and emigrants and stock that preceded McDonald or followed.

Foto is of Virginia L. Stanton and our traveling rig, 1986 style, on the beginnings of the "Great American Desert".

Foto No. 27.   WILLOW SPRINGS.

For the emigrants Willow Springs was a garden spot in this dry, sandy, alkaline stretch of some 52 miles of desert between the North Platte crossing and the Sweetwater River. This place is about 20 miles before arriving at the Sweetwater. Today's traveler sees a grassy meadow, a couple of tumbled down shacks, grazing cattle, antelope, a few willows, a small flow of water and sage brush covered hills. McDonald watered his stock here probably on June 25, 1850.

Emigrant comments regarding Willow Springs: pure cold water, grass, willow grove, discarded possessions - stove, side saddle, burnt wagons, boots, shoes, wagon tires, playing cards.

        ....There has been the greatest destruction of property: wagons, stoves, cooking utensils, clothing, guns, etc. Unless you could see it you can form no conception. Hundreds of thousands of dollars worth of property is laid strewn along the road. We could find anything we want or might want except provisions.........Our load is getting very light and two yoke could haul it but could not travel so fast........

It appears that McDonald, too, has cast his excess to the side of the road.

From p. 34

encamp. Today one sees a tumbled down shed and the few cattle that graze on the grass growing along the trickle of a stream, and the willows still grow.

As the wagons move on westward the process of lightening the load is never ending. **"There has been the greatest destruction of property, wagons, stoves, cooking utensils, clothing, guns, etc....hundreds of thousands of dollars worth of property is laid strewn along the road".** [Let.4, p.3]. The cattle are failing in strength. Their feet are worn from crossing the Black Hills. This road of sand doesn't help them. The dust and heat continues wearing on the strength of man and beast. Poison water has reduced the numbers of draft stock and weakened those remaining. The emigrants and their teams continue to plod on their weary journey. **"The road is sandy and dusty. The wind raises a cloud of dust and sand filling the eyes and mouth. It is very disagreeable traveling. To help the matter, the road is strung with teams keeping the dust stirred up. To say the least this is a mind tearing (and) body tiring road."** Let.4, p.2].

"We reached the Sweetwater River, about 52 miles from the (North) Platte River and have been traveling up it since or near it." [Let.4, p.1]. Upon arriving at the Sweetwater River these thirst starved travelers must have enjoyed a refreshing drink and dip into this **"very rapid mountain stream."** [Let.4, p.2]. The emigrants next turn toward the west again, travel two or three miles upstream to the INDEPENDENCE ROCK, this, the most prominent land mark on the Mormon-Oregon-California Trail. This was a favorite site of early western artists to show the circled wagons of the encamped emigrants. Most every emigrant carved or chiseled or painted his name somewhere on the face or top of this great monolith. Only a few of the names on the rock have survived the elements.

Seven miles upstream from Independence Rock, the Sweetwater River

passes through that famous cleft in the Rattlesnake Range known as DEVIL'S GATE. There is no passage for wagons through the cleft, and the trail necessarily passes around the end of the Rattlesnake Range a short distance to the south. Devils Gate and Independence Rock are perhaps the two best known landmarks along the McDonald Trail.

(The SUN RANCH lies on the west of and adjacent to the Devil's Gate. My wife and I were most fortunate to meet Mr. Sun and to have him show us the wagon traces through his ranch).

The McDonald Trail traverses somewhat along the Sweetwater River and Valley until within 9 miles of the Continental Divide, crossing the river 7 times in the 110 miles from Independence Rock to that pass over the Rocky Mountains. At one point there is a rather strange phenomenon located between 5th and 6th crossing of the river, an ice slough or spring, a place where the emigrants can dig 10 or 15 inches below the ground surface and strike an Ice layer. Many diarists report having a cup of ice water.

"Grass has been scarce the most of the way from Ft. Laramie. We have to drive our cattle two and three miles from the road which makes it laborious to man and beast and slow traveling" [Let.4, p.2]. The combined traffic of the Mormon-Oregon-Calif. Trail can only be guessed. One thousand wagons with 4000 to 6000 head of stock in every 22 mile stretch of trail and each day needing feed, it is a wonder there is feed even within 3 miles of the trail.

Fatigue and sickness are taking its toll on the strength of McDonald and company. "I suppose you have heard reports of the dreadful sickness on this road....but we have always been a little in advance of the worst of it, I think....Isaac and myself had a slight touch of this diarrhea. We took medicine at the

start....(Dr.) Park has had a good deal of practice with first rate success" [Let.4, p.2]. (Isaac, though ill, survived the trip to Sacramento City. He took passage on a ship at San Francisco to return home via Central America and New York. He died enroute and was buried at sea. Isaac's family never quite forgave James McDonald, though he was utterly without blame).

On the night of July 3, 1850, McDonald and company encamp 11 miles before SOUTH PASS. **"We have been in sight of snow-capped mountains for the past week. The Rocky Mountains in our front are white as sheep except where it is blackened by pine and cedar"** [Let.4, p.2]. The following day, Thursday July 4, they travel through South Pass to PACIFIC SPRINGS, the first waters that flow to the west. **"The summit is a gradual ascent and descent. The road does not run over the high part of the mountains which, on the north about 10 miles, rises pretty high"** [Let.4, p.2]. Many emigrants envisioned a great cleft in the Rocky Mountains through which the trail would pass and were much surprised at the ease of crossing over the summit of this great range of mountains.

At Pacific Springs (3 miles west of South Pass) was water and grass and a favorite place for recruitment for emigrants and their stock. Postal arrangements had been made by private courier, for 50¢ a letter, to take mail back to the "States". The Post Office was probably a barrel staked down at the spring to receive the letters. The mail departed Pacific Springs on July 14, 1850 and arrived in Weston, Missouri in late Mid-August. McDonald used this postal service to mail letter No. 4 that he completed on July 5, 1850.

On the morning of July 6, 1850 McDonald and company depart Pacific Springs on the trail westward after recruiting for a day. At 9 miles they cross Dry Sandy Creek. At 15 miles (from Pacific Springs) they **"reached the forks of the road on the 7th (of July,**

1850) at noon. At this fork, the left leads by the Salt Lake, the other the Sublet (Sublette) Cutoff....We took a vote on which of the roads to take. The majority was in favor of the Fort Hall or Cutoff road" [Let.5, p.1]. McDonald and company turn right onto the Sublette Cutoff. In about 5 miles they arrive at the Little Sandy River where they encamp for the night of July 7, 1850 to feed and rest their cattle in preparation for crossing the desert ahead of them.

On the 8th of July they move ahead 6 miles to the Big Sandy River, the last water available for the next 45 miles across the Little Colorado Desert. **"We thought to lay by till next morning....(but) some of the company were impatient and concluded to start that afternoon..."** [Let.5, p.1]. (McDonald and companions no doubt possess a guide book with some misinformation regarding distance across this desert. They believe it to be 35 miles when it is actually 45 miles) They travel all the night of July 8 and do not arrive at the Green River until three O'clock the afternoon of July 9. The stock were exhausted and thirst-crazed from the extra 10+ miles of pull. **"One of our steers gave out and laid down. We got the balance through, but this was a sore drag on them"** [Let.5, p.1]. It was the wise driver, that upon sensing that the stock "smelled" the Green River, unhitched and turned them loose before they stampeded over the bluffs to water with wagon and all. **"We stopped two days to rest our cattle, paid $7 to get our wagon ferried over. Here we picked up a stray ox, a very good one. This fitted out one team again"** [Let.5, p.1].

"We had now to cross some high, rough and steep mountains getting over to Bear River, but we got down the worst by locking both wheels and tying a rope to the hind axle tree and holding back by hand" [Let.5, p.1]. The Sublette Cutoff rejoined the Oregon Trail near present day Cokeville, Wyoming in the Bear River Valley. The emigrants think themselves to be in a garden as they

Continued on p. 77

Foto No. 28. SWEETWATER RIVER.

..........We reached the Sweetwater River, about 52 miles from the [North] Platte River, and have been traveling up it since or near to it.......

Foto is looking east from atop Independence Rock. The Oregon Trail meets the Sweetwater River about 2 miles distant and there, perhaps, McDonald and Company refreshed themselves and their stock on 25 or 26 of June 1850.

PRICKLY PEAR found on all these deserts.

Foto No. 29.   SWEETWATER RIVER from Independence Rock.

This view from atop Independence Rock is up the Sweetwater River and Valley toward the west. Somewhere in the foreground McDonald forded the Sweetwater River and proceeded westerly, skirting the granite hills [Rattlesnake Range] that lie ahead, distant 7 miles.

ONCE A WAGON.

Foto No. 30.   INDEPENDENCE ROCK.

........I could tell you something about Independence
Rock.........etc., but I have not time.......

Independence Rock is the most prominent landmark on the McDonald trail -- Oval
in shape, 1900 feet long, 700 feet wide and about 130 feet above the plain.
The Sweetwater River [in foreground] passes on the westerly and southerly side
and about 100 yards distant from the rock. Camera is looking downstream. The
rock is covered with names. Looked for McDonald name but no luck.

Independence Rock is
mentioned by all
diarists, mountain men,
explorers and map makers
[John C. Fremont in
1842-3], artists [Wm. H.
Jackson].

JUNE 9, 1850 A. Collins
and T. Pauls.

Foto No. 31.   DEVILS GATE.

........I could tell you something about........Devil's
Gate, etc., but I have not time........

Devils Gate is another landmark on the McDonald Trail. This fissure in the
Granite Mountains, through which the Sweetwater River pases, is about 370 feet
deep, 1500 feet long and 50 to 100 feet wide at river level. Camera view is
to the east and downstream on the SUN RANCH, 7 miles west of Independence
Rock. McDonald would have encamped very near here the night of Wednesday, June
26, 1850.

Foto No. 32.   WIND ERODED strip of the OREGON TRAIL.

Edgar W. Stanton, III great grandson of James McDonald, is standing in this
sandy, wind-blown strip of the Oregon Trail. Mr. Sun, third generation owner
of the SUN RANCH, very kindly showed me the Oregon Trail through his property.
Flow of traffic is toward the camera.

Some emigrants cut up
their wagons and made
carts.

Foto No. 33.   OREGON TRAIL and SWEETWATER RIVER.

The Oregon Trail lies on the camera side, and adjacent to, the trail marker and fence [on the SUN Ranch]. McDonald footsteps ??? on the trail from right to left on about June 27, 1850. The meandering Sweetwater River flows left to right. This view is about 8 miles upstream from Devil's Gate.

OX YOKE at Ft. Hall mock-up, Pocatello, Idaho.

Foto No. 34.   SPLIT ROCK.

Split rock, a prominent landmark not mentioned by McDonald. It lies west of Devil's Gate about 12 miles. The Sweetwater River meanders left to right and unseen between Split Rock and camera. The foto was taken from beside the Oregon Trail. McDonald and Company passed behind the camera from right to left.

The Mormon Trail and the Oregon-California Trail joined at the north bank of the of North Fork crossing of the Platte and the combined Trail remained so until the "Parting of the Ways", 19 miles west of the Continetal Divide.

Foto No. 35.   SWEETWATER River Valley.

.......If the cattle's feet would not wear, we could get along as fast as any kind of teams. The horse and mule [teams] pass [us] every day but they must stop to grass longer than cattle and we pass them in return.......if the road keeps sandy and heavy rolling the packers will leave us, which the most of the mule and horse teams are now doing, leaving their wagons. Some ox teams are cutting up their wagons, making carts to lighten and ease their way of traveling.......

Today's view of the serenity of the meandering Sweetwater River, as it flows through this valley, belies the days of 1850 as one thousand wagons per day from the combined travelers of the Mormon Trail and Oregon - California Trail passed through this scene. Those emigrants with half starved and exhausted stock plodded onward. Emigrant diaries mention the great numbers of animals [mostly oxen] dying and covering the trail and the campgrounds with their bloating and rotting carcasses. Today, if this be a campground, there is no sound of cursing drivers or of cow bells or music or laughter or shouting or clanging of cook kettles or sight of camp fires or lanterns of burial parties on the hillsides or stench of dead oxen. The trail lies this side of the river and McDonald traveled right to left.

Foto No. 36. "11 MILES FROM SOUTH PASS".

Dear Mary:

This is now the evening of the third of July. We are 11 miles from the South Pass on the pass over the Rocky Mountains. Three miles from that is the Pacific Springs where the first waters flow to the West. We are all well and if health is spared we will reach there tomorrow [Thursday July 4, 1850]. I expect to mail this there.........Grass has been scarce most of the way from Ft. Laramie. We have to drive our cattle two miles from the road which makes it laborious to man and beast and slow traveling.........We travel about 20 to 22 miles a day. Continual dropping will wear a stone. Just so, continual fatigue will tire a man. I wonder our cattle stand it as well as they do.........

This area is about ½ mile from the Oregon Trail and 11 miles before South Pass. Perhaps McDonald fed his stock here on the scarce grass or willow browse the night of July 3, 1850, or perhaps there was no feed or water to be had. McDonald and Company are half the distance to the California gold fields and the hardships are telling on man and beast. There are another 1000 miles of deserts and mountains yet westward. The endurance test lies ahead.

Foto No. 37.   SOUTH PASS, Summit of the Rocky Mountains.

.........The summit is a gradual ascent and decent. The road does not run over the high part of the mountains which on the north about 10 miles rises pretty high and are covered with snow is no rarity.......The wind rises about 9 or 10 o'clock in the morning and generally blows hard till near sundown......The road is sandy and dusty. the wind raises a cloud of dust and sand filling the eyes and mouth. It is very disagreeable traveling. To help the matter, the road is strung with teams keeping the dust stirred up. To say the least this is a mind tearing, body tiring road........

This foto is toward the southwest. The continental divide and Oregon Trail intersect at the swale in line from camera to center of the left mass of Pacific Butte and distant 1 mile [beyond the burned over sage brush showing in the foreground]. Emigrants traveled left to right. In 1842 John C. Fremont crossed through this pass, referring to Pacific Butte as "Table Hill". AND James McDonald and Company crossed through this pass on July 4, 1850.

Foto No. 38.   PACIFIC SPRING, first waters flowing west.

.........This is now the morning of the 5th [Friday July 5, 1850]. We have laid by at the Spring for a day or two to rest our cattle........This is the last chance I will have to write till we reach our place of destination........Estil publishes to leave St. Joseph with an express on the 15 of May.......He then changed his publication to start an express every 12 days, which he has done. He charges 50 cents a letter to fetch or take a letter to the States........but I am glad to have the opportunity to send you one........The mail starts back for the States on the 7 th of July.......The wind shakes the wagon so that I cannot write........

Estill's express and mail was scheduled to depart Pacific Springs on July 7 but departure date was moved to July 14, 1850. Christopher Ritson and John T. Shortridge departed Pacific Springs with the eastbound Estill express and mail on that date. This mail arrived in Weston, Missouri to be post marked about August 15 or 16, 1850.

Charles T. Stanton [member of the Donnar Party] noted on July 19, 1846.....
....came to a fine spring.......the first water that flows westward.

This foto is taken from the hill at the lower end of the marshy meadow, toward the buildings at the springs. South pass is 2 or 3 miles beyond. McDonald encamped somewhere on these hillsides the night of July 4 and 5, 1850, departing July 6 for the Little Sandy River crossing.

Foto No 39.   WIND RIVER RANGE of the ROCKY MOUNTAINS

          ....We have been in sight of snow - capped
mountains [Wind River Range] for the last week. The Rocky
Mountains in our front are as white as sheep except where it is
blackened by the pine and cedar. I could tell you much of the
scenery and flowers if I were there. I think I will enclose some
little ones in this letter for "Maggie" [Margaret McDonald, his 5
year old daughter].......

Foto is of the Wind River Range of the Rocky Mountains, Lying to the north of
South Pass "about 10 miles". There is but little snow on these mountains as
this year [1987] is a dry year. This view is from near the trail between Dry
Sandy and Parting of the Ways.

Foto No. 40.   PLUME ROCK.

This remarkable piece of nature's sculpture lies a short distance north of the Trail and about 7½ miles before the "true parting of the ways" and 9 trail miles west of Pacific Springs. This natural and colorful edifice, sculptured by the elements, was not mentioned by McDonald. He passed near this point on July 6, 1850.

JULY 1850

S	M	T	W	T	F	S
		1	2	3	4	5	6
7	8	9	10	11	12	13
14	15	16	17	18	19	20
21	22	23	24	25	26	27
28	29	30	31			

Foto No. 41.   DRY SANDY.

The Dry Sandy crossing is mentioned by some diarists but not by McDonald.
It is as its name relates, dry and sandy. There are some stagnant pools after
heavy rain, but no water here to rely upon. Those forced to encamp here dug
pits, hoping to use subsurface water that might seep into them.

This is dry, sandy and alkaline country. The emigrants found most of these
pools to be heavily loaded with alkali and the water poisonous to the stock.
This was not a popular campground.

Foto No. 42.   TRUE PARTING OF THE WAYS.

San Francisco, Sept. 26, 1850

My dear wife:

        ....I will now give you a somewhat detailed account of
our travel. I will commence at the Pacific Springs, the last
place I wrote from on the Plains........We left [Pacific Springs]
on the 6th [of July, Saturday] and reached the forks of the road
on the 7th [Sunday] at noon. At this fork the left leads by the
Salt Lake, the other the Sublet Cutoff. Here, H. Park joined us.
He had been absent nearly a week. We took a vote on which of the
roads to take. The majority was in favor of the Fort Hall or
Cutoff road........

The parting of the ways lies 17 miles westerly from Pacific Springs. McDonald
and Company took the right hand road, hoping to save 50 miles of travel. The
Trail from the North Platte crossing to this bifurcation of the road has had
the combined traffic of the Mormon Trail and the Oregon-California Trail. The
left hand road goes to Fort Bridger and Salt Lake, and the right hand road is
the Sublette Cutoff. A Surveyor's brass monument marked "True Parting of the
Ways" is set at the iron stake [at the forks].

Foto No. 43.   LITTLE SANDY RIVER CROSSING.

........We drove about 5 miles to Little Sandy Creek. We now stopped to feed and rest our cattle as we had to cross a desert said to be 35 miles.......

McDonald and company encamped at the Little Sandy River the night of July 7, 1850. This was the first water west of Pacific Springs [17 miles] that was drinkable by stock and humans. Probably they had to drive their stock up [or down] stream several miles to find feed.

The Trail crosses the Little Sandy River near right-center of the picture and climbs the rise out of the bottom on the cattle trail.

Foto No. 44.　BIG SANDY RIVER.

　　　　　　　.........The 8th of July [Monday] moved to Big Sandy, the last water. This was reported to be 12 miles but proved to be but 6 miles. We thought to lay by till next morning but as the distance was so short, and but 35 miles across, some of the company were impatient and concluded to start that afternoon and get through by daylight.........

McDonald's information [or misinformation] must have come from one of the guide books available for purchase from certain stores in St. Louis. One of the emigrant guide books gives the distance from the Little Sandy to the Big Sandy as 12 miles and distance from the Big Sandy to the Green River as 35 miles.

The Big Sandy crossing can be at the far end of the bluffs or the near end. Travel is from right to left. On these flat plains the teams spread out where possible to avoid the dust that is ever present where wagons and teams travel. This area is a rather famous camping area and last place for filling the water containers before crossing the Little Colorado Desert.

Foto No. 45.   GREEN RIVER near Le Barge, Wyoming.

...........But this 35 miles proved nearer 55 and we did not get through until 3 o'clock the next day [Tuesday, July 9, 1850]. One of our steers gave out and laid down. We got the balance through but this was a sore drag on them. Then crossing Green River, a deep, rapid stream and cold, [swimming these streams] chilled the cattle and we think gave them the hollow horn, a disease the cattle were all troubled with more or less. We stopped two days to rest our cattle, paid $ 7.00 to get our wagon ferried over here.........

McDonald and company, as with many other companies, were misguided by erroneous information in their guide books as to distance across The Little Colorado Desert. The additional 10+ miles gave some companies and their teams considerable distress. There was no water available except from the casks filled at the Big Sandy. As the teams approached the Green River and could sense the nearness of water, it was necessary to unyoke or unharness these thirst crazed animals and let them loose to prevent them from racing wildly over the bluffs with wagon and all.

The Camera is looking up the Green River toward the ford. In August, when the flow is low the ford was in use. With higher water, several ferries were available. McDonald paid $7.00 to ferry his wagon over from right to left.

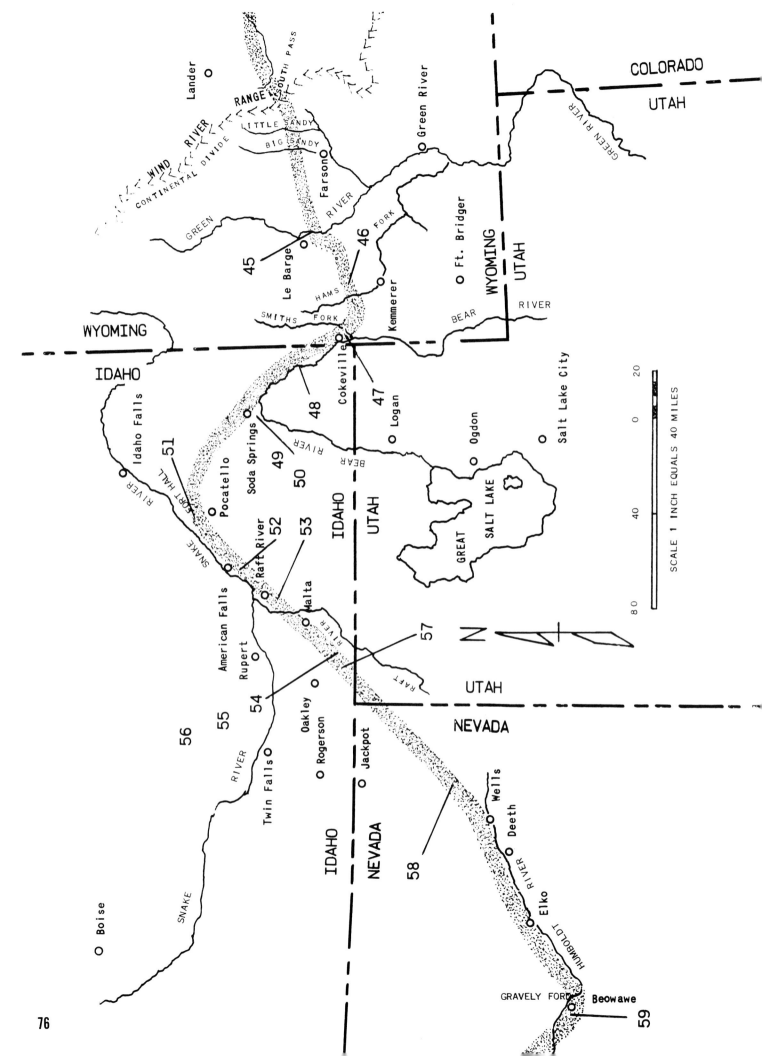

COLORADO

UTAH

Lander

WIND RIVER RANGE

SOUTH PASS

CONTINENTAL DIVIDE

LITTLE SANDY

BIG SANDY

Farson

Green River

GREEN RIVER

GREEN RIVER

45

Le Barge

46 FORK

Kemmerer

Ft. Bridger

WYOMING

UTAH

WYOMING

IDAHO

SMITHS FORK

HAMS

Cokeville

48

47

Logan

BEAR RIVER

Idaho Falls

51

Pocatello

Soda Springs

49

50

BEAR RIVER

IDAHO

UTAH

Ogdon

Salt Lake City

20

0

40

80

SCALE 1 INCH EQUALS 40 MILES

SNAKE RIVER

FORT HALL

Raft River

52

53

American Falls

Malta

RIVER

GREAT SALT LAKE

Rupert

RAFT RIVER

57

N

UTAH

NEVADA

54

55

56

Oakley

Rogerson

Jackpot

IDAHO

NEVADA

Twin Falls

SNAKE RIVER

58

Wells

Deeth

Elko

HUMBOLDT RIVER

Boise

GRAVELY FORD

Beowawe

59

76

From p. 57

travel north, down the Bear River Valley "generally on a good level road" [Let.5, p.1], for the next 58 miles to "the springs" (today, Soda Springs, Idaho).

"July 20th (Saturday) reached the Springs 4 miles from the place of leaving the river......There is an Indian town here or trading post. The Indians are very civil. Some could talk broken English. We stayed till the 22nd as there was good grass.....Four miles from here there is what is called the Hedge Pass (Hudspeth's) Cutoff, but we took the Fort Hall road. The Indians said the other was a very bad road" [Let.5, p.1&2]. Four miles from "here" McDonald turns to the northwest on the Fort Hall Road. He is 1140 miles from St. Joseph.

Twenty miles from the springs the travelers arrive at the Portneuf River and proceed up river 9 miles before turning west some 32 miles to Fort Hall. Although the name and place "FORT HALL" holds a very important place in history, (ranking with Ft. Kearney, Ft. Laramie, Ft. Bridger and others), McDonald mentions only "the road by Fort Hall" [Let.5, p.2] and must have had no need to stop. At the Snake River (only a mile from Fort Hall) the road turns westerly, along the south side of the Snake for about 42 miles to the mouth of the Raft River where the California Trail turns to the southwest and departs the Oregon Trail.

For McDonald and company the next 60 miles up the Raft River valley and through the city of Rocks are rather uneventful. The Hudspeth's Cutoff travelers have joined the California Trail 5 miles before the City of Rocks. This area (City of Rocks) is a most spectacular site. It consists of a field of fractured rocks that are scattered over an area about 4 miles by ½ mile. These rocks are all shapes and sizes, giving the impression of there being a city with its church spires and domed meeting halls etc. The exit from the City of Rocks for all wagons is between

two giant out croppings of rock separated enough for one wagon and its team to pass through. In another mile the Salt Lake Road joins the California Trail in Junction Valley and now those travelers, who have driven the cutoff roads, are all back together on the main California Trail. McDonald has completed 1300 miles of his journey with 650 miles remaining to Sutter's Fort at Sacramento City.

The position of all the emigrants has deteriorated considerably. To their death list is added mountain fever (probably rocky mountain spotted fever). There are companies that have misjudged on food requirements and are now without. There are those who, for various reasons, have lost all their stock and abandoned their wagons and are afoot and destitute. Some are buying their existence while others are begging or stealing, anything to keep moving and stay alive. For those who have "seen the elephant", it is much too late to alter course.

The trail now leads McDonald southwesterly for 100 miles--out of southern Idaho, through the northwest corner of Utah, into Nevada and the **"head of The Humbol(d)t or Mary's River"** [Let.5, p.2], that all important lifeline for the next 288 miles (Wells to Lovelock, Nevada). These are 288 miles of monotony, heat, dust, failing stock, sickness, fatigue and Indians. After the long and seemingly endless travel of 1400 miles from St. Joseph, these weary men and animals must endure new hardships they have not yet tested. It is the Indians that are giving the emigrants new worries. These are not the kind of Indians for which it is safest to "Circle the Wagons". These are called Digger Indians and are found to the north of the Humboldt. Their style is quietly to steal stock out of feeding herds at night beyond the camping areas, and if there are guards posted, to shoot the stock with arrows. These wounded animals necessarily are abandoned. There are occasions when, after darkness, a "jumpy guard", while watching his stock, would fire (by mistake) on

Continued on p. 94

James McDonald, a cabinet maker by trade, made this hat rack with buffalo horns.

Ox yoke at Ft. Kearney blacksmith shop.

Stain on this Wyoming marker is caused by cattle rubbing on it.

Foto No. 46.   HAMS FORK of the Green River.

In this foto the camera looks from the east toward the west, across the Hams Fork valley. Hams Fork lies at the base of the bluffs beyond the feeding cattle. The antelope that were in this scene didn't stay around long for picture taking. McDonald makes no mention of crossing this area other than "high, rough and steep mountains".

PONIES. Virginia L. Stanton and her friends in Hams Fork valley, 1987.

Foto No. 47.   SMITHS FORK of the Bear River.

Behind the camera lies the Bear River valley. If McDonald did not enter the Bear River valley from this gap in the mountains [Smiths Fork], he met the old Oregon Trail that came up from Ft. Bridger about 3 miles south [right of camera]. He then turned North, passed behind the camera and traversed down the Bear River valley, crossing Smiths Fork as he closed on the Bear River. This foto was taken from the outskirts of Cokeville, Wyoming and near the Idaho-Wyoming line.

WAGON   FRAME   at   Ft.   Hall mock-up, Pocatello, Idaho

Foto No. 48.   BEAR RIVER.

          ....We had now to cross some high,
rough and steep mountains getting over on to Bear River, but we
got down the worst by locking both wheels and tying a rope to the
hind axle tree and holding back by hand. We met with no accident
except broke our front hounds. It was a stiff tongue, the worst
fault our wagon had. However, we found a wagon thrown away. It
had a falling tongue. We took the hounds and applied them to
ours which worked admirably, detained us about 2 hours.   We
traveled down Bear River, generally a good level road........

Foto is of the Bear River and valley. This valley was a garden for the
emigrants. Good water, grass, fish, waterfowl and game animals were abundant.
It was a relaxing attitude that came over the emigrants after those
exhausting, long, hot, thirsty and dust overwhelming miles. The great
complaint of these travelers has now become "the mosquitoes".

Foto No. 49.   DRY CONE at Soda Springs, Idaho.

.........July 20th [Saturday] reached the Springs [at Soda Springs, Idaho] 4 miles from the place of leaving the river. These are a curiosity. They burst up out of the ground and run off forming a rough porous rock...... with an aperture at the top and center for the water to boil and foam and spout out. As there are a number of these mounds in the vicinity that are dry, the water has run for a time and left for some other place leaving this rock mound to mold and decay........

Foto is of a dry mound found [Sept. 1987] at the western edge of the Soda Springs golf course. It is the only one we found still "standing". Near by is a spring that oozes some little flow. Ginger checked the taste and declared it "not fit for human consumption".

Foto No. 50.   SODA LAKE at Soda Springs, Idaho.

.........There are two springs coming out side by side separated by a rock. One is clear, the other brownlike tan ooze. This last comes out from under the rock and when you put your head under and draw your breath thro the nose it flies to the head like hartshorn. I could say much more but have not room or time.........There is an Indian town here or trading post. Some could talk broken English. We stayed until the 22nd [Monday, July 22, 1850] as there was good grass........ Four miles from here is what is called the Hedge Pass [Hudspeth's] cutoff but we took the Fort Hall road. The Indians said the other was a very bad road and not much nearer.......

On Saturday, July 20, 1850 McDonald and Company arrived at "The Springs", [near the town of Soda Springs, Idaho]. A man made lake [Soda Lake] has now drowned nearly all this natural phenomenon. These springs were a most unusual and spetacular sight to the tired emigrants.
The camera looks toward the West. The Oregon Trail follows along the base of the hills on the right for about 4 miles, passing into the valley, just beyond the last hill and opposite Sheep Rock [the dark mountain at left]. Upon entering the valley the Hudspeth's Cutoff continues toward the west to join the California Trail near City of Rocks, whereas The Fort Hall Road turns right toward the North. McDonald and Company departed "The Springs" July 22, 1850 and took the right hand fork toward Fort Hall [this fork near the town of Alexander, Idaho].

Foto No. 51.   FORT HALL MONUMENT on Fort Hall Indian Reservation, Idaho.

McDonald refers to Fort Hall only in the statement "the road by Fort Hall". Fort Hall dates from 1834. In 1837 Hudson Bay Company became owners and maintained this as a trading post until it was abandoned in 1855. Other than very high prices for a few salable items it seems to have had little to offer the travelers of 1850. McDonald must have been unimpressed as he did not mention having stopped or having passed it by. Fort Hall does have a place in history and ranks with names such as Fort Bridger, Fort Kearney and Fort Laramie. At the least, in 1850, it was a prominent landmark to all pioneers.

This foto is of the monument marking the site of Fort Hall and lies on the Fort Hall Indian Reservation about 12 miles northwest of Pocatello, Idaho. It is in some disrepair and unattended though a newly graveled unmarked road leads directly there.

TEPEE at the museum and mock-up of Fort Hall at Pocatello, Idaho.

Foto No. 52.   SNAKE RIVER, Idaho.

McDonald referred to this river as "The American Fork of the Columbia River". The Snake River has cut a gorge through the underlying rock creating an impasse for the teams to reach water. The trail runs right to left behind the camera about 300 yards distant. This spot gained its notoriety on August 9, 1862 when Indians attacked a wagon company here [300 yards behind the camera].

This scene on the Snake River is 6 miles downstream from American Falls and camera looks down the river. Sage Brush and Juniper trees have been the predominant flora on the McDonald Trail across the Black Hills and along the Snake River.

RATTLESNAKE. These snakes were not to be "treated lightly". [Foto by Stewart E. Stanton].

Foto No. 53.   RAFT RIVER VALLEY, Idaho.

Where the Raft River flows into the Snake River the California bound emigrants turned left [southerly] onto the "California Trail". The Oregon bound travelers generally remained on the "Oregon Trail" moving westerly along the south bank of the Snake River.

McDonald and company turned left from the Oregon route and entered the final stretch of their long journey. The next 60 miles will be with some comfort as the road by which they travel is "good". These emigrants must have turned southerly into the Raft River Valley with a sense of rejuvenation. They were on the California section of the trail at last.

This foto is toward the west, across the Raft River Valley. The Raft River, in this view is at the base of the far bluffs. Today agricultural usage of groundwater [wells and pumping] has lowered the water table and at the upper reach there is no river evident. A local farm resident suggests observing the area after a heavy rain storm and then the course of the Raft River can be seen.

McDonald traveled right to left through this foto on about Saturday, July 27, 1850 [allowing 20 miles per day from Soda Springs].

Foto No. 54.   AMPHITHEATER, CITY OF ROCKS emigrant camp ground.

This great amphitheater was a blessing for the emigrants. It was a famous trail camping place, as it possessed good water and grass and produced a restful scene that made for a good place to "lay over" for recruitment of the traveler and his stock.

The wagon trains that had left the Oregon-California Trail on the Hudspeth's Cutoff at Soda Springs [Idaho] joined the California Trail at the mouth of Cassia Creek canyon, about 5 miles before coming to this site. To the dismay of the "cutoff" travelers, they saved but 30 miles and made no gain in time as they rejoined the same trains they departed from at Soda Springs.

McDonald and Company might have passed this area on about July 29, or July 30, 1850. The Trail is about ½ mile to the right of foto and crosses the mouth of the amphitheater and moves toward the camera.

Foto No. 55. CITY OF ROCKS, Idaho.

The City of Rocks was one of the more spectacular sights of the whole trail. The emigrants likened this array of rocks to a city with its white walls and church spires and castles and domes and buildings of every size and shape. No diarist could not record the splendor of this great bit of natures architectural design and layout.

McDonald says nothing about the City of Rocks, yet he could not avoid passing through here. This foto looks over a portion of the splendor of these few miles. The trail is left of this picture and travel is away from the camera.

AUGUST 1850

S	M	T	W	T	F	S
				1	2	3
4	5	6	7	8	9	10
11	12	13	14	15	16	17
18	19	20	21	22	23	24
25	26	27	28	29	30	31

Foto No. 56.   EXIT THE CITY OF ROCKS.

The California Trail exits the City of Rocks through pinnacle pass, a narrow gap in the scramble of natures rocks. The Trail passes from the camera, westerly, to the left and adjacent the rock mass at right of center. The gap is but wide enough to pass one wagon and team. Pinnacle Rocks [or Steeple Rocks or Twin Pyramids or whatever name emigrants attached] stand guard 300 yards to the right.   Trails West marker C10 is beside camera.

PINNACLE ROCKS or STEEPLE ROCKS at City of Rocks, Idaho.

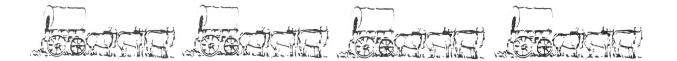

Foto No. 57. JUNCTION of the CALIFORNIA TRAIL and SALT LAKE ROAD.

........The road by Fort Hall was good till we left the American Fork of Columbia River [Snake River] about 60 miles or the junction of the Salt Lake Road.......

Camera stands at the junction of the Salt Lake Road and California Trail. View is toward the east. At near center are the "Steeple Rocks", the only part of City of Rocks seen by those travelers on the Salt Lake Road. Trails West marker No. C11 is plainly visible.

The McDonald statement requires some scrutiny. He is saying that the road was good until they were about 60 miles down the road from the Snake River or to the junction of the Salt Lake Road and the California Trail. This point lies in Junction Valley and is a map scaled distance of 60 miles along the trail, southerly from the Snake River. This junction is the only place along the McDonald route that he specifically identifies between Soda Springs, Idaho and grass at 18 miles above "The Sink" [at present day Lovelock, Nevada].

Foto No. 58.   EAST HUMBOLDT RANGE, Nevada.

.........From that [intersection of the California Trail and Salt Lake Road] to the head of the Humbolt [Humboldt] or Marys River, there is some bad road. This is some 100 miles down [to] the Humbolt [Humboldt River].......

Camera looks south on the California Trail route toward Wells, Nevada. The distant East Humboldt Range has a touch of snow. The Emigrants are enroute to the headwaters of the Humboldt River, the water that flows west and so needed for survival of man and his animals if they are to reach the California gold fields. Prior to the year 1848 this river was called "Marys River". In 1848 John C. Fremont renamed the river "Humboldt River".

The column of emigrants on the California Trail now include the additional traffic from the Hudspeths Cutoff and the Salt Lake Road. McDonald and company have traveled some 1500 miles, and upon reaching the Humboldt, turn westerly and proceed down the north bank of this famous [or infamous] river through this Nevada desert toward the Carson River, 345 miles distant. Their wagon has been lightened to carry only the barest of necessities. The stock that have survived this far are in poor condition, worn by scarcity of feed and water, and excess of heat, dust and strenuous duty. All the emigrants are suffering from exhaustion, and ahead lies their greatest test for survival.

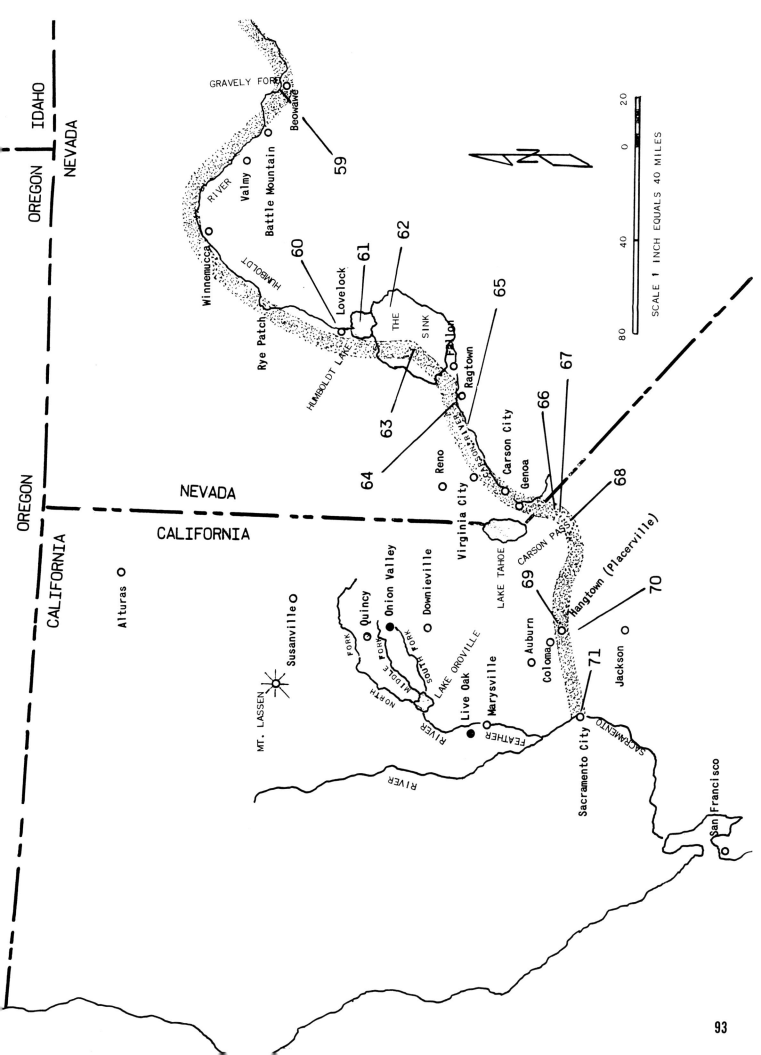

SCALE 1 INCH EQUALS 40 MILES

80   40   0   20

N

OREGON | IDAHO
NEVADA

OREGON
NEVADA

CALIFORNIA

NEVADA

CALIFORNIA

IDAHO

GRAVELY FORD
Beowawe
59

HUMBOLDT RIVER

Valmy
Battle Mountain
60

Winnemucca

Rye Patch

HUMBOLDT LAKE

Lovelock
61
62

THE SINK

63

Fallon
Ragtown
65
64

CARSON RIVER

Reno

Virginia City

Carson City
Genoa
66
67

LAKE TAHOE

CARSON PASS
68

69
Auburn
Coloma
Hangtown (Placerville)
70

71

Jackson

Alturas

Susanville

MT. LASSEN

Quincy
Onion Valley
Downieville

NORTH FORK
MIDDLE FORK
SOUTH FORK
FEATHER RIVER

LAKE OROVILLE

Live Oak
Marysville

Sacramento City

SACRAMENTO RIVER

RIVER

San Francisco

93

From p. 78

another "jumpy guard". On the south side of the Humboldt River is a more belligerent tribe called the "Ute" Indians. These are a more "aggressive" Indian and woe be unto a lone herdsman or hunter caught very far south of the river. More than one wagon has been abandoned for loss of its stock, and more than one soul has gone unburied.

The struggle continues along the hot and dusty trail. Whatever possessions remain are now discarded excepting food supplies and those items necessary for survival. Where most of the stock have died or been run off, wagons are abandoned and the few remaining animals are packed. Those emigrants that have no more stock are forced to back-pack. Not all Indians are suspect in the thievery of animals as some emigrants find theft an expedient means of filling out their teams. The scoundrels that are on the Trail become of increasing concern. Honor to these has long since been cast aside, and they stop at nothing to insure survival. There is safety in numbers and the small units sometime find their security by camping near the larger units.

The Humboldt River can best be described as being a sewer, thick with mud and garbage and rotting stock that have died while searching for browse and grass and water. Many of the these animals become bogged in the mud and are left to die. As this stream flows west it becomes smaller and thicker. When McDonald arrives at the Humboldt River in early mid-August it offers only enough of itself to sustain life. To this add the scorching heat, the fatigue, the dust, and McDonald and his three companions are seen struggling on with their half-starved oxen. Progress is slow. "Our cattle stood it better than we could imagine although they failed considerably" [Let.5, p.2].

"20 miles above the sink (Humboldt Sink) we got good grass. We rested our team and cut grass for feed" [Let.5, p.2]. All wagon companies stop here at these meadows to recruit and cut grass for

stock feed to get them through the next 60 miles. (These meadows are now the lush alfalfa fields around present day Lovelock, Nevada.)

"We left the last place of getting grass on Sunday the 25th (of August). Got to the lower end of the lake (Humboldt Lake) at dusk....with water so bad at the west end of the lake or sink that cattle would do better without it" [Let.5, p.2]. There is a bifurcation of the main California Trail a few miles west, the right hand branch going via the Truckee-Donnar route and the left hand branch being the Carson Pass route. McDonald now enters "the 40 mile desert" onto the Carson route. To men and stock, ahead is a most devastating portion of the entire Oregon-California Trail. The scene along this next 40 miles is of a God-forsaken death march. The stock that worked so faithfully for their owners and were worn to the point of near exhaustion before entering this desert are falling in their traces. These animals are seen in all stages of dying when dawn comes to this desert: The searing heat, the stock unable to swallow any grass for want of water, the dust build-up on and in the nostrils and mouth and throat all take their toll. When the wagons are no longer movable, they are abandoned and the emigrants continue on afoot. There are those, like their animals, dying from heat and exhaustion and thirst and starvation. Many are those emigrants who lie down to rot with their stock. There are few humans with strength or purpose to bury them. The McDonald party survives the struggle to the Carson River. "We had at the desert four yoke of cattle. Four head of these took the scours and on entering the desert they just ran down till they were as flat as your two hands. They gave out before we got across. We got our wagon and two yoke through.....The four sick ones got through the next morning but were so weak they could not travel. We sold them for $26" [Let.5, p.2].

That place where the Trail meets the Carson River is named

RAGTOWN, deriving its name from the appearance created by washed clothing that emigrants laid out on the acres of sage brush to dry. McDonald and companions receive help in getting their wagon and the balance of the team 12 miles up the Carson River to grass. "We there proffered him (the helper) the wagon and balance of team to fetch our clothing through and he was to pay us the difference. Here we had our two horses stolen. We were all much worn down from loss of sleep and travel and did not keep guard.....We here took a change of shirts and some provisions with a blanket apiece on our backs. We had about 240 miles (scales 140 miles) to Hangtown, the first town in the mines [Let.5, p.2 & 3].

The McDonald party walk the Trail up the Carson River to the easterly toe of the Sierra Nevada Mountains, thence south along the toe of the Sierras to the canyon of the West Fork of the Carson, thence up a steep climb to Hope Valley and Red Lake, thence up that dreaded climb over Carson Pass. McDonald and companions had a minimum of problems as they were afoot. There was no wagon to winch and no stock to push.

"We kept our health and had no difficulty in getting along. We got to Hangtown on the 4th of September. On the 5th we bought some picks and shovels and washpans and went to Webber (Weber) Creek, some 6 miles to try the mining.....Sunday (Sept. 8, 1850) .....Benjamin and myself started for Sacramento and hear what mines were in best repute" [Let.5, p.3].

"We reached the city (Sacramento City) on Monday evening, too late to go to the office. In the morning we started to the office.....found a line formed some fifty yards long.....At length I got up and got two" (letters) [Let.5, p.3]. Could this "office" be at Sutter's Fort? Sacramento City marks the end of the California--McDonald Trail. It seems rather anticlimactic to leave this story and James McDonald while he stands in line at

"the office" awaiting his turn to receive his mail. It was but a few days previous that he and his companions were contributing their supreme effort to survive the 1950-mile trek "across the plains" to California and gold.

There are 1950 miles and 119 days since departing St. Joseph, and it has been a long arduous journey for this man who is 33 years old. Though not a scholarly man, he must have been a sound thinking and persevering person who, from his home in New Concord, Ohio and while on the trail, could see beyond the "Elephant" and hold a steady course. He was a rugged Pioneer.

What of Mary who waited at home for that letter telling of "safe arrival at destination"? While at home raising their two children, Anna and Maggie, she endured a 4 year wait for James to return from California with that pot of gold that never was to be his. She too had to be rugged.

Foto No. 59.   HUMBOLDT RIVER at Beowawe, Nevada.

          ....270 miles [from intersection of the
California Trail with Salt Lake Road] in general is a good road
but dusty and disagreeable. The water is bad, warm and muddy.
Grass was good down 200 miles. It then began to get scarce, but
our cattle stood it better than we could imagine although they
failed considerably.........

Foto is of the Humboldt River and was taken in Sept. 1987. Camera looks down
stream at Beowawe about 5 miles below "Gravelly Ford". This year (1987) is
considered a "dry year". The Humboldt River 15 miles upstream from Elko,
Nevada is dry excepting for some few small pools. Gravelly Ford was a most
prominent crossing of the Humboldt and there the trail divided and became
a north bank and a south bank road. The river was crossed whenever anyone felt
the other side was "more promising" to travel. The Ute Indians were more
troublesome on the south side road and the Digger Indians were so on the north
side road. Which road did McDonald travel?

Foto No. 60.   "TWENTY MILES ABOVE THE SINK".

........20 miles above the sink we got good grass. We rested our team and cut grass for feed. We left the last place of getting grass on Sunday the 25th [of August, 1850].........

All California bound emigrants stopped at these meadows for recruitment and to cut grass in preparation for crossing the dreaded "40 mile desert" lying ahead. This is at the location of present day Lovelock, Nevada and today these meadows are producing an abundance of alfalfa hay.

Emigrant wagon traffic at this point has reduced to about 250 wagons arriving from the east and 250 wagons departing for the west, daily.

Foto No. 61.　HUMBOLDT LAKE, Nevada

........Sunday the 25th got to the lower end of the Lake [Humboldt Lake] at dusk. The desert is about 45 miles. Add to this 18 miles from the last grass. [That is] 63 miles without grass and the water so bad at the west end of the Lake or sink [Humboldt Sink] that cattle would do better without it.......

In the above foto the Trails pass left to right, on the south side of Humboldt Lake [at the base of the distant West Humboldt Range] and on the near side behind the camera. At the lower end of the Lake [Humboldt Dike] the Carson Route travelers branched to the left from the Truckee Route and joined with those south side travelers and headed for the Carson River over the infamous "40 Mile Desert".

McDonald and company arrived at the Humboldt Dike at dusk on August 25, 1850. He doesn't say if he encamped or continued onward. One only can speculate as to what the timing and severity of travel on the next 40 miles could bring to to these Carson Route travelers.

Foto No. 62. "THE SINK", Nevada.

Many of the emigrants, hearing of the sink, thought the Humboldt and Carson Rivers terminated in a great hole in the ground. They were much surprised to see them spread out on to this desert and be absorbed by the ground and sun, adding a great lake of alkali to this sun baked 40 miles of desert.

Camera is on the California Trail at the bifurcation of the Truckee and Carson Routes, looking southeasterly across the Humboldt Sink. The "south side" route travelers are moving left to right at the base of the Mopung Hills in the distance. All Carson Route travelers will join at right hand end of the hills and turn south to the Carson River.

Foto No. 63.   40 MILE DESERT, Nevada.

.........We had at the desert four yoke of
cattle. Four head of these took the scours and, on entering the
desert, they just ran down till they were as flat as your two
hands. They gave out before we got across........

Hardly a word from McDonald regarding the suffering of man and beast on this
"40 mile desert". The Trail diarists of '49 and '50 who took time to describe
this God-forsaken event, this 40 mile death march, have given us a look into
the perseverance of man to survive when death hovers near. The heat, dust,
thirst, hunger, poison water, fatigue and sickness laid claim on these
travelers and their stock. This entire Trail was littered with abandoned
wagons and equipment as the stock fell and died in their harness. If a man
fell he was fortunate if there was any one in his Company with the energy or
care to bury him. Many lay down beside the trail to rot with the animals.

This historical occurrence is commemorated by the monument in this foto. It
is located in the desert about 15 miles north of Ragtown and marks the Trail.
Camera looks toward the North with Ginger in the trail.

Foto No. 64.   RAGTOWN, Nevada.

........We got our wagon and two yoke through. But [only] one yoke of these were matched. One of the others [oxen] was very large, the other small. The four sick ones got through the next morning but [were] so weak they could not travel. We sold them for $26.........

Ragtown was at joining of the Carson Route of the California Trail and the Carson River. Here the exhausted and heat struck thirsty travelers and their stock refreshed themselves. The name "Ragtown" came about by the acres of sage and greasewood brush covered with washed garments placed by the emigrants for drying. In appearance and reality, it was a city of Rags.

This foto is of the monument at Ragtown that salutes those pioneers that survived or died in their efforts to cross this hell hole of 40 miles. McDonald again is silent regarding the hardships and dangers of the Trail. We are missing so much by his reticence and his wish not to alarm his family back home in Ohio.

Foto No. 65.   CARSON RIVER, "12 miles up the Carson River".

.........A man that we had been traveling with had some loose cattle. He lent us help to take the wagon about 12 miles up the Carson River [from Ragtown] to grass. We there proffered him the wagon and balance of team to fetch our clothing through and he was to pay us the difference. Here we had our two horses stolen. We were all much worn down from loss of sleep and travel and did not keep guard.........We here took a change of shirts and some provisions with a blanket apiece on our backs. We had about 240 miles [140 map scaled miles] to Hangtown, the first town in the mines..........

Twelve miles upriver from Ragtown places this transaction beneath the Lahonten Reservoir. This camera looks across the "12 mile" spot where exhausted men slept while horses disappeared and where McDonald and company started hiking on their way to Hangtown in the California goldfields.

Foto No. 66. CARSON VALLEY and THE FOOTHILLS of THE SIERRAS.

The Carson Route of the California Trail is along the base of the foothills of the Sierra Nevada mountains in the Carson Valley, about where the cattle are feeding. The trail movement is to the south [right to left] and continues so along the foothills until reaching the West Carson River Canyon, then turns westerly and starts its climb up and over the Sierras. McDonald and his three companions are afoot and not participating in the nearly impossible struggle of getting wagons up this canyon and over its bluffs and rocks with their gaunt animals.

SEPTEMBER 1850

S	M	T	W	T	F	S
1	2	3	4	5	6	7
8	9	10	11	12	13	14
15	16	17	18	19	20	21
22	23	24	25	26	27	28
29	30					

McDonald and companions pass through this scene on about September 1, 1850.

Foto No. 67. HOPE VALLEY, California.

The emigrants emerge from the struggle up the Canyon of the West Carson River into Hope Valley. The West Carson River, as it meanders through this little valley, is but a creek. The scenery of this area is a most refreshing sight to these tired and struggling emigrants who are trying to move their stock and wagons over these high and rugged mountains. It is a place of recruitment.

The travelers of '50 enter Hope Valley from the right of the foto. Camera looks into Luther Pass. CRR trail marker No. 27 is at left of center. McDonald and companions pass near this place on the trail on about September 1, 1850.

Foto No. 68.   CARSON PASS, California.

This foto is at Carson Pass. The large and gnarled trees at the left in the picture are, perhaps, witness to James McDonald and companions as they walk down this westerly slope toward the camera with their sole possessions on their backs, enroute Hangtown [today, Placerville].

This pass was named for famous mountain man and guide, Kit Carson. "His fame [in 1848] then was at its height, from the publication of Fremont's books, and I was anxious to see a man who had achieved such feats of daring among the wild animals of the Rocky Mountains, and still wilder Indians of the Plains.....I cannot express my surprise at beholding a small, stoop-shouldered man, with reddish hair, freckled face, soft blue eyes, and nothing to indicate extraordinary courage or daring. He spoke but little, and answered questions in monosyllables"....
[quotes: William T. Sherman Bib. 15].

Foto No. 69.   HANGTOWN, California.

                              ....We got to Hangtown on the 4th
of September [Wednesday, Sept. 4, 1850]. On the 5th we bought
some picks and shovels and washpans and went to Webber
[Weber] Creek........Sunday Morning we all went [back] to
Hangtown. Isaac and I heard a funeral service in the forenoon.
Then Benjamin and myself started for Sacramento.......

Hangtown was not quite the end of the emigrant trail but it was the
beginning of the gold country. In the year of 1850, when McDonald and
companions arrived here there was a roughened civilization about; a few
stores, a hangman's tree [a bit of law and order ???.], a few places to sleep,
and the usual gambling houses and hangouts of the schemers and camp followers.

This foto is of the Hangtown city hall, a building of late gold rush years.
Hangtown, a small modern city, has but little remaining of the 1850 era to
see. McDonald and companions have added their wee touch to its history.

Foto No. 70.   WEBER CREEK.

.........On the 5th [Thursday, September 5, 1850], we bought some picks and shovels and washpans and went to Webber [Weber] Creek, some 6 miles, to try the mining. We worked Thursday [5th], Friday [6th] and Saturday [7th], got nothing. Sunday morning [8th] we all went [back] to Hangtown........

Foto is of Deane McDonald Stanton, great great grandson of James and Mary McDonald, panning for gold in Weber Creek, down the hill from Hangtown [now called Placerville], California. There are a few colors [specks] in the black sand in the gold pan. Some 12 miles northward James Marshall picked his gold up out of the tailrace of Sutter's saw mill at Coloma on January 24, 1848. James McDonald in September of 1850 found no gold in Weber Creek and in 1987 there remains "nothing".

GOLD. It is this glitter that blinded so many.

Foto No. 71.   "THE OFFICE" at SUTTER'S FORT, Sacramento City, California.

........Sunday [Sept. 8, 1850]......Benjamin and myself started for Sacramento and hear what mines were in the best repute. We reached the city on Monday evening [Sept. 9, 1850], too late to go to the office [Post Office]. In the morning we started to the office........We went on to the office [and] found a line formed some fifty yards long........

This foto is of the office within the walls of Sutter's Fort at Sacramento, California, Feb., 1987. In the foreground are a cluster of McDonald heirs. Sutter's Fort was the terminus of the main emigrant trails leading to the goldfields of California. Today it stands as a monument to all those sturdy pioneers who lived or died in their struggle to reach these walls.

Though McDonald did not mention the name "Sutter's Fort", he did mention "the Office" in Sacramento City. In November 1849 a post office was established in Sacramento City. Sutter's Fort changed its name to Sacramento City and a postal system was established from San Francisco. Is this office and storage building of John Sutter at Sutter's Fort the same as "THE OFFICE" referred to by James McDonald in his quest for Mail?

TRAILS   END

Dear Mary this is now the evening of the third of July we are 11 miles from the south pass on the pass over the Rocky Mountains three miles from that is the pacific springs where the first waters flow to the west, we are all well and if health is spared we will reach there tomorrow where I expect to male this I as I expect you have got a letter from me written from ft Carney & one from ft Laremia I will commence at that place But I will be Brilf we left our incommend on the monday following crossed the Black hills the road was hard and sharp on the cattles feet there feet ware wore to the quick and hindred there traveling some yet we have got along verry well this is over three hundred miles from the ft a great part of the whole road from the fort here is hard on there feet and they are very mutch worn we resort to many expedients to toughen there feet and if the road should turn out fonorable we will go right along so far as that part is concerned well to resume my story, we got to the Ferry on the north Branch of plat river on friday 9 oc 110 Miles from the Laremia ft there is a ferry 30 miles a Bove this place But the emigrants rode forward to see what chance there was to crofs they returned and said there was somany they would not get across for ten days we concluded to try it here altho there Boats ware very inferior we had a tight wagon bed when we started But it had shrunk and would take some time to make it tight we therefore Bargained for five Dollars to take our wagon and load oher which was done By 1. oc Isaac and I went over to load up the wagon and the rest of the Boys staid to drive the cattle over they worked hard till night and did not get one of them over the horse that sim Shively was riding got to swiming and floating forhe

THE TREK

OF

JAMES MacDONALD

NEW CONCORD, OHIO

TO

CALIFORNIA

1850

SECTION II

FORWARD to SECTION II

December 22, 1930

Dear Aunt Jeanne: (Janet).

    Last fall, when I was in Ames, (Iowa), I found that Aunt
Maime (Mary) had several letters written by Grandfather MacDonald
while he was on his first trip to California. I feel that now
they are of real historical interest. I have had them copied and
expect to have them printed in the form of a little booklet for
members of the family and a few libraries. What I need now is a
little sketch of his life........

                                    Don

                    Edwin MacDonald Stanton

    In April, 1949 my uncle Don visited here at Live Oak,
California. At that time he told me of these letters and what he
had thought about the booklet. I added my enthusiasm to his and
in about 1951 came my copy.

    Section II is the original booklet of letters and some
family history. Three letters written by James McDonald while
in California to my grandmother, "Maggie" (Margaret), are
added as are the photographs of the outside of letter No. 6 and
of head stones and Onion Valley and James with cow.

                                    EWS, III

Introduction

The years embraced by the life of James MacDonald, and particularly those years of his active adult life, cover one of the all important periods of American history. These years cover the period when all of that vast territory from Indiana to the Pacific and from Duluth and the Canadian border south and westerly to the Mexican border was transformed from the land of the Indian and the buffalo and the Great American Desert into Iowa, Kansas, Colorado, California and nineteen other states essentially as we know them today.

This period also embraces many of the great civilization changing inventions of the nineteenth century. The steam railroad came into significant development. The telegraph, the telephone and electricity, as we know it today, began to take its place in the world. Barbed wire, which did so much to transform the prairie, came into general use. The great revolution in agricultural machinery got well underway. In fact, the first reaper and binder to be used in Southern Iowa was first demonstrated in 1883 on the farm then occupied by James MacDonald near Mt. Pleasant, Iowa.

The histories of this period give much space to the more colorful characters. Names such as Fremont, Bridger, Kit Carson, Sutter, Young of Chicago and many others are blazoned on the pages of history. James McDonald may have a wee place in the history of California because at one time he served as Secretary of the Vigilantes where they were establishing law and order in the golddiggings. Marysville was their headquarters and each time I go there I stop at the oak tree where my grandfather told me they hung those destined to be hanged.

While James MacDonald was not of the type to become a famous character of Western history, he was a typical representative of those sturdy, God fearing, hard working and sound thinking pioneers who did conquer the West and who, in the aggregate, did very largely determine the kind of country it is today.

The several letters written home by James MacDonald while on the long trail to California and from California, along with the letters of his wife, Mary, to him while in California, give not only a picture of material things as they were in those days, but also of the inner thoughts, the mental attitudes, the heartaches and the worries of a devoted couple.

In this little booklet those letters are included along with other data concerning James and Mary MacDonald in the hope that they will be not only interesting but inspiring to his grandchildren and their children.

Edwin MacDonald Stanton
Schenectady, N.Y.
March, 1951

BRIEF HISTORY of McDONALD FAMILY

Transcript of letter from Mary [called Maime] Woodruff MacDonald Knapp Ames, Iowa [without date] to Dr. Edwin MacDonald [called Donald] Stanton, Schenectady, N.Y., oldest son of Margaret Price b. 1845.

JAMES McDONALD: Should have been MacDonald, the family Scotch, coming to U.S. from Glasgow, probably about 1816.

Born: May 5, 1817 in Rahway, New Jersey - of a large family, the others having been born in Scotland, all except a younger brother, Andrew. Other and older brothers William and Archibald Sisters: Katherine, Janet, Mary.
Father: Archibald MacDonald.
Mother: Margaret Orr MacDonald.

Moved West, unknown date, settled in Muskingum County, Ohio. Mother died. Stepmother, of proverbial type, sent the two young ones [sons] still at home, adrift and James learned the cabinet makers trade with his sister Katherine's husband----Wintermute in Zanesville, Ohio. Andrew learned the Tailor's trade. These two brothers were never far separated in life, coming with their families together to Iowa in Spring of 1863.

Married: Mary F. Grumman, youngest daughter of Isaac and Jamima Price Grumman -her family having moved to Guernsey Co. Ohio from Newark and Elizabethtown, N.J. Her family came to U.S. before the Revolution, early probably, from the Island of Guernsey off the coast of England. The story has it that James & Mary F. MacDonald were the "handsomest couple in Muskingum County" at time of marriage - he black hair and eyes, active and of good repute; she, black curls, dark eyes.

Children: Margaret Price   1845   It is not difficult to trace
            Anna Eliza   1848   the names of these children
            Florence Grumman   1855   to their sources. The
            Edwin Archibald   1858   Woodruff in my name going
            Mary Woodruff   1860   back to New Jersey
            Janet Orr   1863   relatives.

California: Across the Plains with ox teams and covered wagon, walking most of the way. Left St. Joseph, Mo. May 13, 1850. This was the place of embarkation of the overland groups of gold seekers. Here they were fitted out with whatever was lacking in their previous preparations, and from this point they really took up the long trek.

Incidentals of possible interest: His letters to his wife make little mention of the hardships; and in this are perhaps disappointing. It is not hard to find the reason. He dared not tell her, anxious and worried as she was, because of this undertaking of his. Isaac was Isaac Walters, mother's nephew, a young man devoted to [his] Uncle James [and] who went on this

expedition in spite of protests of father and sisters, his mother recently dead at the time. He suffered with others from diarrhea caused by the water they had to use, was ill when they got through and begged to be sent home. Father put him on a boat at San Francisco to return via Panama. He died enroute and was buried at sea. The family never quite forgave, tho utterly without blame, my father.

The man, Hugh and Dr. Parks are the same. Ben is Ben Metcalf, married to mother's niece Mary Ellen. They are evidently not in the best of humor with each other.

Father was gone on this first trip to California four years. Returned by boat San Francisco to Nicaraugua, across and up the east coast to New York by boat, train to New Concord.

His second trip to California was made one year or so later to look over property he had left with man to attend to, getting no returns; found the party was appropriating income and he had to go back and see to it. He went this time via New York by boat to the Panama, across the Panama and up the West Coast to San Francisco. Later, up into the Oregon Country and the head waters of the Missouri River. Took flat boat [Herman says steamboat] at Ft. Benton and came down the Missouri to Nebraska City. Over into Page County Iowa to his brother, Archibald, who had come to Iowa meanwhile. He brought him to Ft. Des Moines [Father never ceased calling that city Fort Des Moines] and by stage to Iowa City where the R.R. West terminated in that day.

He was not gone long this time as I suppose. If as a child, I had listened well, I might have definite knowledge of all this time. His tales, hair-raising tales of the Rapids, the Indians on the shore as they came down the river - calling - "Come <u>over</u> here!" and they must go - appease them with food or beads or something or they would meet them at a bend of the river lower down and be not so easily dealt with.

Father's California trip was successful financially, tho I think he dug little gold. Prices out there were fabulous and he used his trade; sawed off the legs of a table and pocketed $ 10.00 for the job, etc. He lost on sheep brought West, the story of many men, even of Herman's father.

Your mother, devoted and serious-minded even as a young girl, left Muskingum College a Junior [I think] when the family came West - finishing in the Mount Pleasant Female Seminary in 1868. She kept our father going financially and was to the younger children an example and a beloved sister - companion, mother. I can almost never think of her without a prayer to this day.

Aunt Maime

Muskingum College: one of the very many educational institutions for which Ohio is noted. The Alma Mater of many prominent men and women, situated at New Concord, Muskingum Co. Ohio. Birth place of the MacDonald children, all.

William Henry Harper, first President of Chicago University, a graduate- with many others of note, and a student there when your mother was.

Important: Herman [Herman Knapp, husband of Mary] wants I should be sure to say that Father's return, the first trip, was on the same boat with John C. Fremont & party from San F. to New York. Fremont's book, the Pathfinder, would give date, etc. 'Twas no doubt the winter of '54 & '55.

M.

50th Wedding Anniversary
James and Mary McDonald 1893
Taken on the front porch of "The Maples"
Ames, Iowa. Campus of Iowa State University

Front row: l to r. Mary [Grumman] McDonald, Margaret McDonald Stanton, James McDonald; back row: Florence McD. Wishard, Mary McD. Knapp, Edwin McDonald, Anna McD. Waugh, Janet McD. Chipman.

Ames, Iowa 29th March, 1951

Dr. Edwin MacD. Stanton
Schenectady, N.Y.

Dear Don:

In reading over the letters of Grandpa and Grandma MacDonald and the account which mother wrote to you some time ago, I am tempted to add what seems to me to be a connecting link of our childhood on the campus.

It seems to me that it should be mentioned that the MacDonalds lived a few weeks with your family at the Maples and then a while at Woodruff Place and that during those visits or periods Grandpa used his hands at his bench in the basement of the two houses to make corner cupboards and side boards such as our mothers were proud to have in the house. I remember a step ladder into our attic and chairs and such that were very useful.

While he was working I am sure that at least one of us asked a lot of questions and I remember that I was turned off many times with a treat of red cinnamon candy that was so hot that it kept my tongue busy for some time. Sometimes he would lean against the work bench and tell us yarns about the trek across the plains in 1850 and one I remember the best was about his hunting for fresh meat as they Journeyed West. He told that he walked most of the way to California and that the only time that he could ride was in the early morning while putting the pans and kettles in the right place in the wagon. They were in too big a hurry to be off to do that work standing still and he seemed to have been the main cook. One day as he hunted some distance from the trail he came over a rise and a herd of Buffalo saw him about the same time that he saw them. At first he moved away slowly and they just watched him, but then they began to walk toward him so he walked a little faster. They ran slowly at first and then faster so he had to run fast too. He headed toward a low place where the grass was high and as he reached it he fell on his knees and crawled at right angles with the travel of the herd as fast as he could make it. He heard them coming and he crawled faster yet. Finally they passed within a very few feet.

When your mother passed away in 1895 you will remember that our family moved into the Maples with yours and that the grandparents were there too, which made a rather large family. Most of the time there were from 12 to 15 at the table and two maids in the kitchen. in 1897, when Byron [Knapp] was less than a year old, Mother took all four of us to Oxford, Nebr. to visit. The MacDonalds must have still owned the house on the bluff of the Republican River there and Aunt Anna and Uncle Dick Waugh still lived there up on the hill.

Your Cousin

Seaman Knapp

James McDonald taken in Oxford, Nebraska about 1886.

Prize Holstein.

Interment in cemetery at Iowa State University, Ames, Iowa.

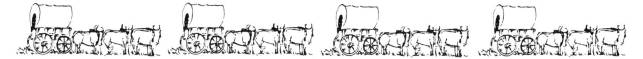

Dear James:

I am going to ask you a few questions. I have heard a great deal about the wickedness of California, and knowing you never enjoyed yourself in society that was wicked and profane, I have often thought [and perhaps you may say I think about things I need not] how you spend your time, whether you were, owing to your situation, compelled to join with the rest. Now, dear James, don't think for a moment that I have thought or think that going to California has made you a wicked man. No, far from it, I would rather think it has been a trial and a lesson that has brought you closer to Christ. Oh James, I think of these things. I have not forgotten the talk we had the night before you left home, and the resolution, or I might say the vows, we made in the presents of God as all things are known to him, if you were permitted to return to your family the different life we would lead. Oh that we may not become weak but grow stronger in faith. Now, James, I think if you were to make any pretensions towards that walking in the path of duties you would meet with opposition by your companion. I know he is not the kind of a man to be agreeable company for you, but oh don't let such company blind you that you lose sight of a Savior or the mercies of God. You have never mentioned any of your difficulties on your way there or since you got there. We have heard of Ben's fighting with Hugh and threatening Issac and scoffing and pointing at him when he read his Bible. Whether this be true of not, I can't say but if it was I know it gave you trouble. These things are not public talk. I would like to know whether Ben lied or if it is true. Now I dont wish you to leave Ben as it regards your business. I think him the best man you could get, but you know him better that I do. All I want is to know how you get along with him and if he was really ugly to Isaac. These things John Walters knows nothing of, we are told.

Oh James, do not think hard of me for writing so to you and asking you so many questions. If you can or think worth while to answer them, do so; if not, think no more about it. Speak of this to no one in your letters except myself. This you had better burn.

Mary

James, I have not said one word about your coming home. I know you will come as soon as you can without my urging you. Oh, but I would love to see you again.

Mary

the interests of good, you have sometimes may if your appreciates on
your way there or since you got there, we have heard of Ben's fighting
with Hugh and threatening Isaac and scoffing and sneering at him
when he read his Bible, whether this be true or not I can't say, but if it
was I know it gave you trouble, these things is not pleasant talk, I
would like to know whether Ben is dull or weak it is true, now I want
what you could get, but you know how better than I do till I seemed as
to know how you get along with him and if he was really ugly to
these things father knows nothing of we mentioned him, I know
do not think there if one for writing so to you or asking you so many
questions of you can or think it worth while to answer them do so if
not think we care about it speak of this to no one in your letter
except myself, this you had better burn

Mary

As for I have not seen one word about your coming home
I know you will come as soon as you can without very
urging you. Oh but I would love to see you again

Mother

St. Joseph, Mo. May 12, 1850

Dear Mary:

It is now nine o'clock at night. I am writing on our table by
the side of our tent. It is my turn to watch the cattle. It is
necessary to keep a guard as there is a great deal of stealing
done in this place. They steal horses, mules and cattle in one
part of the town and sell them in another. Two men will join and
have a team of horses or cattle - one will take them and sell
them and slip off, the other will come up and claim the property,
state that it had been stolen, prove it and take it. Such games
and all other kind of rascality are carried on here with a high
hand. We have bought four yoke of cattle - very good ones for
which we paid $300. We will buy another yoke in the morning
which is all we will get. We have one pony and perhaps will get
another - this one we paid $40 for. Perhaps some will wonder
why we did not get mules before we left Kentucky or Illinos.
When on the river we got the prices of them along the river and
out in the interior, which prices ranged from $80 to $ 300 - in
fact, well-broken mules could not be bought within the compass of
our pile. We can do as well in buying stock here as anywhere but
all other things are enormously high. Mules are plenty here but
too young to stand the hardship. We therefore thought it
prudent to buy cattle and it is the prevailing opinion that
cattle are the safest. We have seen a great many that have
returned and this is their opinion but they are not so fast.

Issac and Hugh went down to Weston and Kansas last week to buy
corn, ponies and cattle but bought nothing but one pony. They
saw Mary Jane Lattimore there as smart as ever. William had
started for California the week before. She gave each of them a
money purse. Isaac got a letter there from you. I was very glad
to hear from you; would have liked to have known where you were
going to live in Concord; if you have not a comfortable house, I
would rather you had stayed if you had been satisfied. I have
pretty strong hopes of returning in a year. There have been a
great many in these parts who have returned and with from 3 to 7
and to 20 thousand. But generally from 5 to 7. All things
appear tolerably favorable. The season is backward which throws
us late of starting and the grass will not be as good as if the
season had been early and the number going may make it scarce.
This was one grand reason why we chose cattle and these are, we
think, the principal difficulties we will have to contend with.
There is no grass yet except along river bottoms and low marshy
lands, and these are not plenty enough to supply stock and travel
steady. But we have bought ground corn enough to feed, we think,
till there is plenty of grass if it comes this year. We will
start tomorrow sometime in the day to try the traveling. We are
camping now two weeks. It goes pretty well. We all eat pretty

hearty of baker's bread, fried ham, molasses and coffee. This we have one day and the next we have coffee, molasses, fried ham and bread. But that is nothing if we did not think of home. If I knew all was well, I think I could go through with a light heart, but I will hope that it is so. I expected to get an answer to the letter I wrote from St. Louis, which if there had been no delay, would have been time. There is no mail from the East since last Wednesday. There will be one on Monday. That is tomorrow at 5. Perhaps one of us will stay back till evening. I got two letters out of the office here, one for William Vrie, the other for Catherine McDonald. I knew they had gone or would leave Kansas before they could be remailed there. I took them out and will take them with me. If I see them all is right, if not, they are as well with me as in the office. We heard through John Keerans of the death of James White and that it was very sickly in Concord last, if accounts be true. There are two cases of smallpox in town. One is an emigrant, the other a citizen - the former is getting better. There are a great many returning home again from here. Some found things higher here than they expected and have not money enough to purchase an outfit. Others are discouraged. Some are robbed of all they have and can't go. Others try gambling and lose their all and are obliged to return. It is said that this town resembles California much, only business is not done on so large a scale. Had we known when in St. Louis what we knew when here two days, with capital we had, we could have cleared two thousand dollars in three days by laying it out in corn and oats. Corn was 50 cents in St. Louis and here $ 1.50 and $ 1.75 and at Council Bluffs $ 4.00 per bushel. Oats are now selling at $ 3 per sack, $2\frac{1}{4}$ to $2\frac{1}{2}$ bushels in a sack. There has been a rise in the river and grain has been shipped up. It will be down to 75 cents in a few days as the most of the companies have crossed the river and camped out. Some are now 10 and 12 miles out and feeding and browsing their stock. It is said by some of the returned Californians that we will meet several returning trains. If so, I will not fail to let you know how we are getting along. We will write from Ft. Kearney at all events and perhaps the Pacific Springs - as it is published there will be an express mail to return from there after the most of the trains have passed. We cannot tell when we will get through but I want you to write once a month regularly. Let the first be sent so as to be there by the first of September. At all events give it two months to go and then write once a month from that first; direct Sacramento City, upper California. My opportunities will not be as good as yours but I will improve all chances and be as regular as I can.

I can think of nothing more of business matter to write. We do not realize before starting from home the value of that home. The value of a peaceful home, if ever so humble, is infinitely more valuable than all the golden dreams that man's fancy can

invent. When I think of the shortness of life and the few necessaries really required, I think it folly for a man to torture his mind and that of his friends, even for a short time, for all the difference a few dollars can add to his or their comfort or satisfaction over and above the necessaries which a man that wills is sure. But perhaps this is enough philosophy. I think there are few that would leave home if they could realize it in its extent before they started. But these fits are worst when I sit down to study or reflect. There is one thing that bears a man up. Everything is excitement from one extreme to another - all bustle and run. It is a perfect frolic all the day, and at night we are ready to go to sleep. It is thus the time is pushed along. Do not think there is anything like turning back, for that is not the case, but as I said, I think few would start if they could realize it in time. All are in good spirits. Isaac, I think, is the most down but he will get over that, I think, when we start. I would like to know how you are fixed, if Mamie is still going to live with you which I know she will if you have a house to suit. I think I see Mamie sitting with her arms folded looking down and Anna leaning against her knees. Poor Maggie, too, where is she? Bless her life. She is sleeping for it is now 1 o'clock. The night is a little cool but not uncomfortable. Tell Maggie she must lift Anna up when she falls and fetch in wood to Mother and when she gets to school she must try to learn so she can read to papa when he comes home. Maybe she can teach Anna to read a little too. If she is a good girl, I will fetch her and Anna something pretty.

There has one month passed since we left home. The time seems short, too, considering. I must close and bid you goodbye for a season so good night, may God be with you and preserve your health. Kiss the children often for me but do not indulge them too much. Take great care of your health. Elizabeth gave me, through Andrew, a most excellent book,"Polak's Course of Time". It, with some other books, I have passed the time very agreeably.

Mary, farewell for this time.

J. McDonald

Ft. Kearney, May 30, 1850

Dear Mary:

We are now in sight of the Fort and all are well and have been well. We left St. Joseph, as I stated in my last, on the 13th [Monday] about 4 o'clock in the evening. We went up the river 5 miles and crossed in the morning, early. We have had no accidents or trouble. We are now about 300 miles from St. Joseph. It is now about eleven o'clock. The health of the emigrants is generally good. There is some sickness and a few deaths, but it is light considering the number on the road. As far as we have seen the prospects are better than we expected. Grass is plenty and our cattle are all thriving except one steer. He seems too clumsy to travel, but we think he is thriving these few days as we have had him tied back and we carry him often. The balance of our cattle are fine. It is frequently remarked by men as we pass, "There is a team and wagon that will go through".

I am writing in the open prairie. I would have written last night, but Dr. Park was called back in the afternoon to set a boy's leg. The boy fell out of a wagon and it ran over him. The hind wheel was locked and crossed his legs up at the thick of the thigh and broke the left leg, and I had a concern to make to set his leg in with a joint under the knee that the leg might be kept stretched to prevent its being shorter than the other. I think the job was done about as well as it would be done in the States. It took us till late in the night. The boy is being hauled on the wagon. His father, sister and brother are along with him. He will certainly have to endure everything if he lives at all.

I must now tell you something about the road which surely is the finest in the world. There are some bad places at creeks, etc., but on the whole is the loveliest, smoothest road I ever saw. I had no conception. You can see in all directions for miles and miles. It is nearly level. Some places it is rolling, and in general, more or less looks like one vast field or meadow. If you see a spot you conclude it is an animal and name it by its size and color. We have seen some buffalo and several antelopes. Some of the companies have killed of both kinds. If the journey is no harder than we have seen, it is nothing. Our feet get a little sore and we often are some tired. We have five good yoke of cattle and two good ponies. We get along nice. The time slips past faster since we started than I could have imagined.

I must tell you about our meat biscuit. It is splendid. One of the little cakes makes a pint of soup of which we are all very fond. We laid by on both Sundays, and expect to do so throughout, if we can make it suit for wood and water. We have been in company, for a week past, with a man by the name of

127

Cleveland of Missouri Sta., and perhaps will keep with him if we like his company and he ours.

There is much more I would like to say, but our mule team has gone ahead and I must be brief. I will write more fully at Ft. Laramie, 337 miles from here. Dr. Park went back the morning of the 14th [Tuesday] for letters to St. Joseph and got one for me and A.B.M. Tell Mary Ellen A.B. is well and in good heart. He says he will not write till he gets to Ft. Laramie. My love to all - goodbye.

Your affectionate husband,

James McDonald

Isaac sat on the same tuft of grass and wrote to his father.

Platte Bottom, June 13, 1850

Dear Mary:

As this is my watch night I thought I would occupy a part of it in writing to you. The boys all talk of writing from Fort Laramie and we do not expect to stop long there and our time even when laying by is in a good part taken up in tending to the cattle and horses. I thought I would occupy this lonely hour. It is raining a little and I am sitting in the wagon. The wind shakes it almost too bad to write.

As I wrote from Ft. Kearney I will commence there. We passed it on the 30th of May, encamped six miles west. There are two or three frame houses. The balance are made of sod cut into square blocks and built like stone. There is no timber of any note. On the islands in the Platte there is some cottonwood and willows but of an inferior quality. For the first 200 miles up the Platte, there is but little variation of scenery. The river is from $\frac{1}{2}$ to 1 mile wide, studded thick with small islands. We laid by on Sunday [June 2, 1850] about 45 miles from the Fort [Fort Kearney]. In the afternoon we heard there was a man by the name of Clapp encamped on the other side, on the Mormon Road leading from Council Bluffs. Metcalf and I swam over to see him but it was not the man we wanted. The river is from six inches to 6 feet deep, the bottom quicksands. The water runs rapid and muddy, boiling like the Missouri. We forded the south Fork of [the] Platte about 4 o'clock the 5th of June. The water was from 1 to $2\frac{1}{2}$ ft. deep; the bottom, quicksands. We could not let the cattle stop as the sand would settle away and our wagon go down. The river is from $\frac{1}{4}$ to $\frac{1}{2}$ mile wide. This crossing is about 23 miles above the forks of the river [Platte]. We crossed over the Bluffs about 3 miles to the North Fork [of the Platte River]. Sunday, June 9th, laid by from 1 o'clock. We left in the morning on account of bad pasture. June 10th we passed an Indian encampment the first we have seen since we passed a place called the Agency 30 miles from St. Joseph. The scenery on the Platte so far is much of a sameness; what can be said of one mile can be said of it all. Bluffs on one side, the river on the other. The bottom is from 5 to 8 miles wide [with] no timber except, except as I said, on the islands and occasionally a small red cedar in the hollows of the Bluffs.

June 12th [Wednesday], passed another Indian encampment. They were pulling up stakes to move. Their tents are made of buffalo hides, tanned for the purpose, and sewed together with thongs. They are made in the shape of a cone. They have pine poles shaved smooth. These are tied in a bunch about 15 ft. from the butt, then they are set on end and the butts spread out to form the shape, and the hides stretched on and pinned down to

the ground. In moving, the women take and lash two or three of these poles on each side of their ponies [of which they have a great many] letting the hind end spread about 6ft. and drag on the ground. On these they place an oval crate made of willows and in this they place their baggage, their children, young puppies and quite young colts if they have any. The women drive. Some others follow. The men ride in front or behind. They have a great many dogs, a number of which are harnessed in the same manner and loaded according to size. The Chiefs have briefs from the officers of the forts stating the friendship and good behavior of the chiefs and asking a little bread, sugar , coffee, flour, etc. as a compensation for the whites driving the buffalo from the river, etc. Our pasture has been poor for the last 100 miles, yet we cannot perceive the cattle falling away much. Some of the heavy ones are getting their feet tender by wearing off. We passed another Indian village today. There are some white men among them. one has a blacksmith shop. We get the use of it to make some ox shoes and nails. Hugh and Jim stopped and we drove on. Hugh caught up at noon but Jim stopped to cut and weld the tire of a wagon for George Wilson. He is on the road for California with his wife and son. I called to see the lawyer at Glascow that Ichabod had to do his business. He said it could not be made of Wilson at present but it was in such a way that it could be got if he was ever worth it. Perhaps Ichabod could send the papers to Benjamin or W. Shannon and yet have it secured. Stoner & Oldham Co. we have not heard a word of since we left; If they are ahead, I wonder we have not seen their names written on some tree or card, as it is the common way of letting those who are behind know where they are. But we have not seen a single name belonging to that company.

We saw Calvin P. McDonald of Concord June 5, 1850 on a tree in ASH HOLLOW. We passed it on the 8th [Saturday]. We saw J. Day & Co. about 400 miles back. There was a man in the train that they belong to who was sick. They laid by him when we passed and we have not seen or heard from them since. We are now about 35 or 40 miles from Ft. Laramie. We expect to get there day after tomorrow. We will then be out from St. Joseph five weeks and have made a distance of 641 miles. The health of the emigration is quite different now from what it was when I last wrote. Since we have been on this river sickness has been increasing, principally diarrhea. Some die very suddenly with it. It is by some called the cholera, but we think not. I suppose it is occasioned by drinking the water of this vicinity. The ground is often covered with a whitish substance called an alkali, but it is a mistake. The water that falls on the ground and collects in pools becomes so hard directly it will not wash a bit, whereas an alkali would break and soften the water. Yesterday we passed by some splendid scenery, landscapes, Court House Rock, Chimney Rock, Castle Bluff, Scotts Bluff, etc. These

I would describe but I have not room.

This is now Saturday, the 15th [of June, 1850], 8 miles west of Ft. Laramie. We have encamped for the purpose of staying until Monday. We passed the fort at 12 o'clock. We had to drive out here to get pasture and will take out letters back to the Fort. They keep a register of names, number of men, women, horses, mules, cattle, wagons, etc. We there found the names of Mc's boys, Cambridge boys, Evansburg boys and all we wanted. The Norwich boys, Day & Co. are encamped about 2 miles behind. C. P. McDonald and Company and the Cambridge Company are about 12 or 15 miles ahead. We expect to overtake them in two or three days. We have gained $2\frac{1}{2}$ days on them in the last 150 miles. I must now give you the number that have gone and had their names registered. There had passed on the 14th [Friday, June 14, 1850] 23,293 men, 363 women, 375 children, 6,345 wagons, 18,436 horses, 5,955 mules, 14,072 oxen, 1,689 cows. How many have passed and not gone and had their names put down we cannot guess. From what we have seen, we think about two thirds are now passed. How many have gone the Mormon trail we cannot even guess. I must now tell you [that] you have no idea of the immense crowds who are traveling this road. There were about 1,200 wagons passed the fort last Thursday, 900 or 1,000 today and the crowd thickest behind us. It will continue but for a few days. A. B. Metcalf was taken last Sunday with diarrhea and was very bad for 2 [or] 3 days but is now much better. He says he will try to write in the morning, but he thinks his hand will tremble too much.

O, Mary, the time seems long and tedious when I look back at home, home sweet home, but so much of my time is occupied in hurry and push and drive that the time slips by almost afore I ken, at least much faster than I anticipated. It is a long time since I left home, but any other point on the route, Wheeling or Cincinnati, seems but yesterday. I try to give myself but little time to think of these things. I believe I get along the better for it, with the exception of the thoughts of you and the children, and while I have my health I think the hardships and privations, at least what I have seen, as nothing worth mentioning, altho we see some almost every day going back discouraged. We have seen nothing to discourage us, yet there is a good deal of sickness and deaths on this river. This diarrhea cuts them off sometimes in a few hours, but we will try to meet it promptly and trust to God for consequences. I think often of you all and wish you knew how well we are getting along. I think you would not fret. We are well fixed for the trip. If we have our health and the roads and pasture continue as good as we have had, we will get through in the month of August, but we dare not calculate as we know nothing of the roads or pasture.

had, we will get through in the month of August, but we dare not calculate as we know nothing of the roads or pasture.

Tell Maggie [that] Papa will try to come in the spring but he does not know if he can or not. Bless their lives. I would like to see them. That is my greatest expectation of happiness as far as this world is concerned is meeting you all once more. "Roll on, Sweet Moments, Roll on and Let the Poor Pilgrim Go Home, Go Home". I hope you have a comfortable house for you and mama. Do not stint mama or yourselves in comforts while you have the means to get them. I hope to be able to assist you within the year. If I don't get home, my paper is getting done. I do not know whether I can write to you again or not before we get through. Perhaps I can from Pacific Springs or Fort Hall. If I can, I will. I will expect some letters as soon as I get through. I may write a letter partly and have it ready to fold and send it back by some returning wagon.

Good night

James McDonald.

Letter 4, page 1

Dear Mary:

This is now the evening of the third of July [1850, Wed.]. We are 11 miles from the South Pass on the pass over the Rocky Mountains; Three miles from that is the Pacific Springs where the first waters flow to the West. We are all well and if health is spared we will reach there tomorrow. I expect to mail this there. As I expect, you have received a letter from me written from Ft. Kearney and one from Ft. Laramie. I will commence at that place but I will be brief. We left our encampment on the Monday following [June 17, 1850], crossed the Black Hills. The road was hard and sharp on the cattle's feet. Their feet were worn to the quick and hindered their traveling some, yet we got along very well. This is over 300 miles from the Fort [Laramie]. A great part of the whole road from the Fort here was hard on their feet and they are very much worn. We resort to many expedients to toughen them and if the road should turn out favorable we will go right along. Well to renew my story, we got to the Ferry on the north branch of the Platte River on Friday [June, 21 1850] at 9 o'clock [a.m.] 110 miles from the Laramie Fort. There is a ferry 30 miles [3 miles] above this place but the emigrants rode forward to see what chance there was to cross. They returned and said there were so many they would not get across for ten days. We concluded to try it here altho their boats were very inferior. We had a tight wagon bed when we started but it had shrunk and would take some time to make it tight. We therefore bargained for $5 to take our wagon and load over which was done by 1 o'clock. Isaac and I went over to load up the wagon and the rest of the boys stayed to drive the cattle over. They worked hard until night and did not get one of them over. The horse that Sim Shirley was riding got to swimming and floating for he could not swim and made out to take him, Shirley, 1½ miles down the river. The boys drove the cattle back to the place of ferrying. B. Metcalf was some wet and just getting stout again concluded to come over to the wagon that night for dry clothes. He got on the same boat that fetched our wagon over in company with 11 others. About half way across, the boat sunk. Benjamin swam to shore. Three others swam to shore; some were taken up by boats that went to their relief but three were drowned, two of them good swimmers. Two other men were drowned the same day, one in swimming a horse, the other a mule. The next morning we all went to fetch the cattle, labored until near night, got seven over and gave $1 a head to have the others ferried over. This was Saturday [June 22, 1850]. We drove three miles Sunday [June 23] morning to pasture at the Upper Ferry. They have good boats with ropes stretched across and wagons are not detained one hour. Our informants proved to be men interested at the Lower Ferry and we were detained at least one day and a half. Since we left the Platte River the country has been barren and sandy. I could tell you something about

Independence Rock, the Devil's Gate, etc., but I have not time.
We reached the Sweet Water River, about 52 miles from the Platte
River, and have been traveling up it since or near to it. This
is a very rapid mountain stream and must fall from 25 to 72 feet
to the mile with low banks and narrow bottoms. Grass has been
scarce the most of the way from Ft. Laramie. We have to drive
our cattle two and three miles from the road which makes it
laborious to man and beast and slow traveling. I suppose you
have heard reports of the dreadful sickness on this road. It has
been said there was not as many deaths in St. Louis to the number
of inhabitants at the worst stage of the cholera in that place as
was on these plains. But we have always been a little in advance
of the worst of it, I think. The sickness now is much abated.
Isaac and myself had a slight touch of this diarrhea. We took
medicine at the start. I. Campbell had a pretty severe scourge
but is pretty well past. Park has had a good deal of practice
with first rate success. We have not seen him since since Monday
morning. He stopped back with a sick man, a Mr. Blair of Piqua,
Ohio. We have been in sight of snow-capped mountains for the
last week. The Rocky Mountains in our front are as white as
sheep except where it is blackened by the pine and cedar. I
could tell you much of the scenery and flowers if I were there.
I think I will enclose some little ones for Maggie. Tell her
papa sent them from the Rocky Mts. for her. She must take care
of them and be a good girl to mother. Tell her to give Anna one
little one for me. I cannot send the prettiest ones as they
would be too large. As it is getting late I will stop and go to
bed and finish before I pass the Office.

This is now the morning of the 5th [of July, 1850]. We have
laid by at the Spring [Pacific Springs, Wyoming] for a day or two
to rest our cattle. The summit is a gradual ascent and descent.
The road does not run over the high part of the mountains, which
on the north about 10 miles, rises pretty high and are covered
with snow is no rarity. Here the weather is quite cool for the
season. A man can walk the most of the day with his coat on.
The nights are quite cold. The wind rises about 9 or 10 o'clock
in the morning and generally blows hard till near sundown. It
then falls. The road is sandy and dusty. The wind raises a
cloud of dust and sand filling the eyes and mouth. It is very
disagreeable traveling. To help the matter, the road is strung
with teams keeping the dust stirred up. To say the least this is
a mind tearing body tiring road.

I will give you a description of one day's occupation and
it will suffice with but little alteration for the whole trip.
Commencing in the morning, we rise at daybreak, start a fire,
wash, cook breakfast, take up our tent, fold our bedding and
pack in the wagon [once in two days grease the wagon], eat
breakfast which consists of fried side of meat, sometimes ham, or

dried beef, sugar, coffee, sometimes stewed peaches of which we have pretty plenty. Our bread is either sea biscuit, crackers or biscuit of out own baking. These are generally cold as we have not time to bake in the morning. By 5 or 6 o'clock the cattle are driven in. We then doctor their sore feet, hitch up, pack away our cooking utensils and start. Two of the men take up the long gad, say "Come haw, Taylor and Buck, come here to me". We change drivers at noon, stop, kindle a fire, make some soup of our meat biscuit which, by the way, is the greatest article of food ever brought on these plains. It is worth its weight in gold. Of what we started with, we have not used one-sixth part and we use it once and sometimes twice a day. We shave or pound it up, cover it with cold water, let it soak soft, fill it up with hot water, set it on the fire, boil it and season it to taste, then break some flour in it. It is most excellent. But to resume; we rest about 1½ hours, then drive on until five o'clock. Two commence cooking, two drive the cattle off to water and pasture, Two fetch wood and water, set up the tent, make down the bed. When the men return from the cattle they eat their supper, take their blankets and buffalo robe, go out and watch the cattle till they lay down, then they lay down and sleep till morning, then as before about 5-6 o'clock fetch them in, etc. Once a week we unload our wagon to air our goods. We travel about 20 to 22 miles a day. Continual dropping will wear a stone, just so, continual fatigue will tire a man. I wonder our cattle stand it as well as they do. If the cattle's feet would not wear, we could go along as fast as any kind of teams. The horse and mule [teams] pass [us] every day, but they must stop to grass longer than cattle, and we pass them in return. Mule and horse teams that passed us three or four hundred miles back, we see every day or two and sometimes every day for a week, and some packs that passed us 400 miles back passed us the other day again, but if the road keeps sandy and heavy rolling, the packers will leave us, which the most of the mules and horse teams are now doing, leaving their wagons. Some ox teams are cutting up their wagons, making carts to lighten and ease their way of traveling. There has been the greatest destruction of property, wagons stoves, cooking utensils, clothing, guns, etc. Unless you could see it you can form no conception. Hundreds of thousands of dollars worth of property is laid strewn along the road. We could find anything we want or might want except provisions. There are some that are scarce and ready to buy. Flour is selling for $15 per hundred, dried apples $20 per bushel.

I must mention that the ox I spoke of in my other letter as failing became so stubborn and sullen [that] we had to leave him about 125 miles back. We think we can pick up one as they are left in numbers by the way from lameness and other causes. There are alkali lakes and poison springs that the cattle get into.

Some of them die in a few minutes [whereas] others are scoured and left very weak, but in a few days can be driven on. Our load is getting very light and two yoke could haul it but could not travel so fast. Yesterday evening some of out boys found a board with "C. P. McDonald New Concord passed July 1st in the evening" written on it. That puts him three days ahead of us. That is a day and a half of a gain since we saw his name last. I think he gained that by our delay in crossing the Platte River. George Wilson thought we were ahead of him. We laid by and we have not seen him since. He had a good mule team. The man he was in company with is now behind. The Cambridge boys we have not heard of since we were at the Fort [Laramie]. There are numbers leaving their companies and packing on a single horse. Others pack to take on their backs. There Were six started from here this morning with packs on their backs. It is the opinion of many that it is the only way that the most of the men will get through, but it is not our opinion. We think we can get through and save our team. We have heard many discouraging stories but find them generally false. We pay no attention to them of of late. [We] take our own course and do our own business. When We get through, if that should be, I will write several letters and give my opinion of the best way to get through this country. Many think this will be the last season any will try this route as the prairie grass once eaten down does not grow much the next season.

This is the last chance I will have to write till we reach our place of destination. I am sorry you did not know to have written a letter to this place as I could have had a letter. The mail left St. Joseph the 12th of June. When we left, Estil published to leave St. Joseph with an express mail on the 15 of May. That was too soon for the mail to do me any good but the backwardness of the season kept the emigration back much later than was expected. He then changed his publication to start an express every 12 days, which he has done. He charges 50 cents a letter to fetch or take a letter to the States. I was in hopes you would see the advertisement and send me one here, but I am glad to have an opportunity to send you one. A. B. Metcalf is now writing to his father. He says he will not write to his Mary Ellen now as he promised to write to his father and he has not time to write two letters and his father will take his letter directly out. He is well and in good spirits Mary Ellen would not think hard if she knew our chance to write. I would have written to Andrew and others if I had a favorable opportunity but to lay down my pen every few minutes, the wagon shaking with other inconveniences, I will dispense with it for the present.

Since we left home we have heard many accounts of the mining business by men who have been over before, all encouraging. Whether you can read this or connect it to make sense I don't know but you can try. This is a toilsome journey, but I have seen nothing as yet to prevent my undertaking the same journey if it was necessary. It is or has been very sickly besides other dangers such as I have mentioned. There are many who would not come this far again for all they expect to get. A man with a family leaving home undergoes torture that leaves all other troubles in the dark. But that can be appreciated by none but such as has tried it or been left at home to wait others' return. I expect to receive a letter from you in California in a few weeks after you receive this. Isaac is writing to his father. When you write again, tell me all about everything and every person whom I have ever known. All will be interesting to me. I believe I can think of nothing more that would be interesting to you and will close. Give my respects to all. There is nothing on earth I desire so much as to see my family and friends. I dare not think of them.

Dr. Park has not come up yet. His patient must be bad or he has got into other business. The mail starts back for the States on the 7th of July [Sunday 1850]. It is said to be 700 miles from here to the mines. We have set the last of August to get through. I must close by saying goodbye and may God bless you all. Farewell.

James McDonald.

The wind shakes the wagon so that I cannot write.

San Francisco, Sept. 26, 1850

My dear wife:

I am in the City and well in health. My last hurried scribble I suppose you have or will get before you get this. I will now give you a somewhat detailed account of our travel. I will commence at the Pacific Springs, the last place I wrote from on the Plains. I am presuming you got my letters from Fort Laramie and the Springs. We left the Springs on the 6th of July [1850, Sat.]. This is about 1100 miles from the Missouri River. There was a company from St. Louis that brought out letters from the States and took letters back from the Springs, charging 50 cents each. We left on the 6th and reached the forks of the road on the 7th [of July, 1850 Sunday] at noon. At this fork, the left leads by the Salt Lake, the other, the Sublet [Sublette] Cutoff. Here H. Park joined us. He had been absent nearly a week. We took a vote on which of the roads to take. The Majority was in favor of the Fort Hall or Cutoff road. We drove about 5 miles to Little Sandy Creek. We now stopped to feed and rest our cattle as we had to cross a desert said to be 35 miles. The 8th of July moved to Big Sandy, the last water. This was reported to be 12 miles but proved to be 6 miles. We thought to lay by till next morning but as the distance we moved was so short and but 35 miles across some of the company were impatient and concluded to start that afternoon and get through by day light But this 35 miles proved nearer 55 and we did not get through until 3 o'clock [P. M.] the next day [July 9, 1850]. One of our steers gave out and laid down. We got the balance through, but this was a sore drag on them. Then we crossed Green River, a deep, rapid stream and cold. Swimming these streams chilled the cattle and we think gave them the hollow horn, a disease the cattle were all troubled with more or less. We stopped two days to rest our cattle, paid $7 to get our wagon ferried over here. We picked up a stray ox, a very good one. This fitted out one team again. We had now to cross some high, rough and steep mountains getting over on to Bear River, but we got down the worst by locking both wheels and tying a rope to the hind axle tree and holding back by hand. We met with no accident except broke our front hounds. It was a stiff tongue, the worst fault our wagon had. However, we found a wagon thrown away. It had a falling tongue. We took the hounds and applied them to ours which worked admirably, detained us about 2 hours. We traveled down Bear River, generally a good level road. July 20th reached the Springs, [Soda Springs, Idaho] 4 miles from the place of leaving the river [Bear River]. These are a great curiosity. They burst up out of the ground and run off forming a rough porous rock, which in time, forms a mound some 12 or 15 ft. high of this rock with an aperture at the top and center for the water to boil and foam and spout out. As there are a number of

these mounds in the vicinity that are dry, the water has run for
a time and then left for some other place leaving this rock mound
to mold and decay, which as it molds becomes like yellow ochre.
There are two springs coming out side by side, separated by a
rock. One is clear, the other brown-like tan ooze. This last
comes out from under the rock and when you put your head under
and draw your breath through the nose it flies to the head like
hartshorn. I could say much more but have not room or time.

There is an Indian town here or trading post. The Indians
are very civil. Some could talk broken English. We stayed till
the 22nd [Monday, July 22, 1850] as there was good grass. We had
a pony stolen, we think by a French trader. An Indian came and
told us he could find it for us. He took a horse and one of our
boys took the other pony and tracked the stolen one about 3 miles
into the mountains. [They] found her tied in a thicket. For
this, we gave the Indian some bread. Four miles from here there
is what is called the Hedge Pass cutoff [Hudspeth's Cutoff], but
we took the Fort Hall road. The Indians said the other was a
very bad road and not much nearer. The road by Fort Hall was
good till we left the American Fork of Columbia River [Snake
River] about 60 miles, or the junction of the Salt Lake road.
From that to the head of the Humbolt [Humboldt] or Marys River
there is some bad road. This is some 100 miles down to the
Humboldt. 270 miles, in general, is a good road, but dusty and
disagreeable. The water is bad, warm and muddy. Grass was good
down 200 miles. It then began to get scarce, but our cattle
stood it better than we could imagine **"altho"** they failed
"considerable". 20 miles above the sink [Humboldt Sink] we got
good grass. We rested our team and cut grass for feed. We
left the last place of getting grass on Sunday the 25th [of
August, 1850], [and] got to the lower end of the Lake [Humboldt
Lake] at dusk. The desert ["40 mile desert"] is about 45 miles.
Add to this about 18 miles from the last grass. [This totals] 63
miles without grass and the water so bad at the west end of the
lake or sink that cattle would do better without it. I forgot to
mention, the ox we picked up at Green River got poisoned at the
Soda Springs and died the day we left that place. We had at the
desert four yoke of cattle. 4 head of these took the scours and
on entering the desert they just ran down till they were as flat
as your two hands. They gave out before we got across. We got
our wagon and two yoke through, but one yoke of these were
matched, one of the others was very large, the other small. The
four sick ones got through the next morning but so weak they
could not travel. We sold them for $26. A man that we had been
traveling with had some loose cattle. He lent us help to take
the wagon about 12 miles up the Carson River to grass. We there
proffered him the wagon and balance of team to fetch our clothing
through and he was to pay us the difference. Here we had our two
horses stolen. We were all much worn down from loss of sleep and

travel and did not keep guard. They were stolen by some
California traders that were out buying horses and cattle. At
least, we think so. We here took a change of shirts and some
provisions with a blanket apiece on our backs. We had about 240
miles [closer to 140 miles] to Hangtown, the first town in the
mines. We kept our health and had no difficulty in getting
along. We got to Hangtown on the 4th of September. On the 5th
we bought some picks and shovels and washpans and went to Webber
Creek, some 6 miles, to try the mining. We worked Thursday,
Friday and Saturday, got nothing. Sunday morning we all went to
Hangtown. Isaac and I heard a funeral service in the forenoon,
then Benjamin and myself started for Sacramento and hear what
mines were in the best repute. We reached the city on Monday
evening, too late to go to the office. In the morning, we
started to the office. Going down the street we saw F. Beeham in
the street selling hot coffee cakes and pies at a table on the
sidewalk. Pays $5 per foot per month for the privilege of
letting his table set on a board pavement like Isaac's porch in
Concord. This is for every foot the table is long in front. He
had a long spell of sickness and was not able to work and took
this plan to earn his board. We went on to the office, found a
line formed some fifty yards long. We took our station at the
end. Just imagine my feeling while waiting. Was there any word
from home or not? Beeham had received none. Others told me they
had received none. Such suspense is beyond endurance. At
length, I got up and got two, one dated 23rd of June and one the
24th of July. I broke open the latest date and found it in
Andrew's handwriting. A thought struck me all was not right.
My eyes would not follow the lines for near a minute. Benjamin
stepped up next and got none. He was much hurt and chagrined.
We found but very little difference in the reputation of the
mines. After making all the inquiry we could and listening in
business houses, we found it was altogether a lottery in the
mines. We found that a majority of the miners that were
successful last Fall are not as well off now as they were last
Fall. There are numbers who have been in a year and cannot go
home for want of means. I thought that in my situation that less
wages if sure, would be the best for me. Andrew Grey was getting
$10 a day. I got a promise of a place for Isaac and a prospect
for ourselves We concluded to go back and fetch out things down
and go to work. I sat down to write a few lines to you before I
went back to Hangtown which I have done in haste. A.B.M.
standing over me hurrying me for fear we would not get back.
Mary, still direct your letters to Sacramento City.

Unsigned, letter probably not all preserved.

Union Valley, May 18, 1851

Dear Mary:

I thought I would again endeavor to let you know how and where I am. Myself and Metcalf are well. We are up in the mountains on the headwaters of Feather River. [Author's note: ONION VALLEY is on the headwaters of the Feather River]. The snow is from three to ten feet deep on the north and west sides of the hills. We started for the mountains when we left Sacramento but about that time a snow fell some 8 or 10 feet deep up here and prevented us from coming at that time. We were obliged to lay by till the snow settled. Many perish from cold in the Valley, being from the south. Many had just got up before this storm which was much the heaviest snow that fell this winter. This valley is situated high, being near the tops of the mountains. The nights are cold, freezes pretty sharp. When the sun shines and no wind it is uncomfortably warm. When it is cloudy and windy it is quite cold. In the low valleys, only some three or four miles from here, the snow was but from one to two feet deep and lay but for a few days, and now it is as warm as our June months. This difference of temperature is caused by the difference of altitude in coming out of these valleys to the tops of these hills. It is generally from three to four miles and as steep the most of the way as you can keep your feet to climb.

Robert Leepes is in this place. From him I heard that McDonald's boys had or were about to start for home; also General Moore would leave in a few days. I wish I was ready to go along but I am not. I have not what I came for and it is here if you are so lucky as to get hold of it. Within the last ten days we have heard of the burning of San Francisco. That portion of the city that was burnt is about equal to that portion of Zanesville [Ohio] that is within the boundaries from the sixth street Baptist church to the river south and west. From all accounts they are going ahead again and will have it built up in a few months. My last letter from home is dated the 15th of December [1850]. There are no doubt letters in the city for us but we cannot get them. We could get our letters here if we expected to stay long enough for the return of the messenger. We expect to leave here in a few days. We are going further into the mountains and what our facilities will be to get letters to or from the city, I cannot tell, but should you not get letters for some time be not uneasy on our account. It is healthy in the mountains. We still think we will get it and , I hope, in time to return in good season this fall, but these are only hopes. Time will prove on what ground our hope is founded. I have written but once since we left the city. That was from Dry Creek. Benjamin has written to Mary Ellen.

I wrote from Dry Creek to I. Morton. I requested him to speak to Erastus Scott concerning that mill claim. I am a little surprised that matter was not settled sooner. Erastus said he could collect it in sixty days at furthest and would do it as soon as he could.

It is thought there will be more gold taken out this season than any previous year. Much time and money was spent last season in damming and aqueducting the river which in most cases proved failures and many were hunting something large and made nothing. I have been some among the miners and the mines and I believe to take the whole of the miners as a mass and for a specified time, say one year, and divide the whole amount of gold taken out by the numbers of men employed and it would be about $2 or $2.50 per day. I do not think it would exceed that and it costs $1 per day to live. Some make their 20, 30, 50 and even 100 dollars per day and where that is the case, of course, some must be doing a small business.

I believe I have nothing more worthy of communicating. I will write at each favorable opportunity but they may be far between. I would like to hear from home. It seems a long time since I got a letter. I still feel in hopes you have heard from Isaac Walters. I think it is not possible that that vessel and all belonging to it was lost and not heard from either in the States or here, and she must have been lost between Archipelago and Panama as that letter of Bushfield's goes to show. I need not tell you to remember me to Grandmamma and the children. Give my love to all my friends. I must close, my Mary. I must again say farewell for a season. I hope it may be a short season.

James McDonald

Note: I believe this letter No. 6 should have "Onion Valley" at its heading because the headwaters of the Feather River are in Onion Valley and not "Union Valley". E. W. Stanton, III

ONION VALLEY, headwaters of the FEATHER RIVER.

Foto is of "Onion Valley" at elevation 6200 feet. The ravines along the edge of this valley still show the signs of placer diggings. The mountain peak, with a touch of snow, is Pilot Peak. McDonald does not mention any mode of travel to this point nor his means of keep. He did take the time to write one of his infrequent letters home. The below foto is of the outside of letter 6 mailed by someone that passed through Sacramento City on June 11, 1851, the cost 40¢.

California   August 25, 1851

My Dear Daughter Mother tells me you have been going to Scool and
is Learning to read. ssh tells me too that you are a good girl
and is good too Granmamme and, Anna, pappe is glad to here that
and when he comes home he will fetch something for his girls
pappa is glad to here his girl goes to school and trys to learn
...............can write a letter ....little indian
girls and boys here doo not go to school ....all day they
have no ....and they are brown as little
..........[above portion not readable because of stain] Mr.
Henshaw our nearest neighbor has two little girls very prity
little girls and I gess they are good girls too you must get aunt
Phebe to write you a letter for pappe and tell me what you are
dooing and what Anna does to spend hir time let hir write some
too pappe must finish his letter pappe wants to see his Magge and
Anna very mutch but is too far away he will come home in time
Bless his little girls be good to Granmamma and Mother & all the
rest   your pappe   Mc Donald

          addressed to: Miss Margaret Price

     [address not discernable due to stain damage]

This letter and the following two letters to Margaret Price
McDonald [his daughter] are exactly as written, spelling and all.

                                                    EWS,III

This letter was addressed to: Miss Margaret P. Mc Donald
New Concord
Muskingum County
Ohio

care of
Mary F. Mc Donald   and was post marked Marysville, Calif
Feb 28

California Feb 29th 1852

My Dear Daughter I have been wishing very mutch for a long time
to see you and your little sister Anna I think I can see hir
standing between Grandmothers knees talking prity fast and Rover
too I expect he is in the house sleeping the lazy fellow
I expect mother is sewing and Grandmother is sitting with hir
arms folded smoking hir pipe I wonder if my little girls is
good to Grandmother I would be very sorry if they were not,
Mother says they are pritty good girls I would have liked to
send some little presents to my girls But I cannot get them at
this place but when I come home I will fetch them something nice
you must write pappe a letter and tell him what he must fetch
for you and sister pappe was very sorry he could not come home
in the spring to hiz little girls pappy found two little
pictures the other Day One is for you and the other for Anna
the little dog made me think of Rover and home and the little
girl in the other picture I thought was Anna hideing hir head
under grandmothers apron tell Aunt Phebe she must help you write
and must write some hirself, you and Anna must be good girls
and Doo mutch work for Mother till pappa comes home Bless his
little girls he must bid them good night

your pappa
Jas Mc D

Moors Ranch in California Nov. 9th 1852

My little Daughter

I received your kind letter August the 22 it was a long time
getting here but I was very glad to here from my little girls
again, and I am very glad to see that she learns so well as to
Be able to write so good a hand I am prity well in health and I
think I will get home to see my little girls some time next
summer and sooner if I can I do want to see them very much indeed
you tell me that Anna fights you a goodeel. I am glad you doo
not fight with hir that is like a good girl and I think you are
good to Granmother Phebe & Mother and for that I am going to send
you a little gold dollar in this letter you may Buy just what you
pleas with it the next time you write you must tell me whether
Anna fights you yet Tell hir if she wont fight you any more I
will send hir a gold dollar too in another letter; the wind
Blows hard here too day I think we will have some rain soon we
had one little shower last week all we have had for seven months
it dont rain here in the summer and only about 4 months in winter
is all we have in a year you must write to me soon again and tell
me how granmama gets along and Anna and Rover too is he as
good a Dog as when I left home I expect he is a prity lazy Dog
By this time, I must write some more to mother and aunt Phebe,
you must be a good girl to every Boddy and every person will like
you and be good to you, pappe will never forget his little girls
he has Been mutch longer away from them then he expected and is
very sorry to make it any longer But cannot well help it, May God
Bless my little girls is pappes prayr for you sweet girls

your Father Jaz Mc Donald

M. P. Mc Donald
A. E. Mc Donald

BIBLIOGRAPHY

1......Barry, Louise. THE BEGINNING OF THE WEST. Kansas State Historical
       Society. Topeka, Kansas. 1972

2......Franzwa, Gregory M. MAPS OF THE OREGON TRAIL. The Patrice Press.
       Gerald, Missouri. 1982

3......Franzwa, Gregory M. THE OREGON TRAIL REVISITED. The Patrice Press.
       Gerald, Missouri. 1972

4......Haines, Aubrey L. HISTORIC SITES ALONG THE OREGON TRAIL. The Patrice
       Press. Gerald, Missouri. 1981

5......Harris, Everett W. THE OVERLAND EMIGRANT TRAIL TO CALIFORNIA. Nevada
       Emigrant Trail Marking Committee, Inc. Reno, Nevada. 1980

6......Holliday, J. S. THE WORLD RUSHED IN. Simon and Schuster. New York,
       N. Y. 1981

7......Hunt, Thomas H. GHOST TRAILS TO CALIFORNIA. American West Publishing
       Company. Palo Alto, California. 1974

8......Meeker, Ezra. Ox-TEAM DAYS ON THE OREGON TRAIL. World Book Company.
       Yonkers, N.Y. 1922

9......Moeller, Bill and Jan. THE OREGON TRAIL, A PHOTOGRAPHIC JOURNEY.
       Beautiful America Publishing Co. Wilsonville, Oregon. 1985

10.....National Geographic Society. TRAILS WEST. National Geographic
       Society. Washington D.C. 1979

11.....National Geographic Society. THE ITCH TO MOVE WEST. August, 1986.
       National Geographic Society. Washington D.C.

12.....Oregon-California Trails Association. THE CALIFORNIA TRAIL. Oregon-
       California Trails Association. Independence, Missouri. 1986

13.....Oregon-California Trails Association. OVERLAND JOURNAL.
       Oregon-California Trails Association. Independence, Missouri.

14.....Paden, Irene D. THE WAKE OF THE PRAIRIE SCHOONER. The Patrice Press.
       Gerald, Missouri. 1985

15.....Sherman, Gen. William T. MEMOIRS OF GEN. W. T. SHERMAN. Charles L.
       Webster and Co. New York, N.Y. 1891